Equiano

Let me to lay before you the following true story. It tells of what the slave trade inflicted upon my people. For it was this trade which tore me away from all that is dear to my heart. Yet this cruel destiny has also caused me to know the modern world, in all its wonder. Above all, it taught me to have faith.

Chapter 1

My childhood home

My name is Olaudah Equiano, although I have had many names.

My mother and father gave me my true name. Men who owned me gave me other names. Now, I can use my true name again, for I am free.

I am just an ordinary man, though I have seen extraordinary things. I was born in Africa, enslaved as a child and brought to America. I was then taken to England. I now write my story as a free man in the great city of London in this year of 1789. Millions of my countrymen have been made slaves. I have been far luckier than most.

I will tell you my story, but do not think me vain for telling it. I do not expect praise or glory. Nor do I seek pity. But if my story serves humanity in the smallest way, my heart will be at peace.

I was born in Eboe, a small province of the African kingdom of Benin. It was the year 1745, though we did not know it.

I was blessed to enter the world in one of the most fruitful and charming parts of the kingdom, the valley of Essaka. Our valley was lush, green and overflowing with trees, fruit and grasses. It was far from the sea, which we had never seen. It was also far from the white man, who we had never seen.

We lived simply, but well. The king was far away, and we were our own masters. The elders were our leaders and our judges. My father was an elder of our tribe. They called him an *embrenche,* a nobleman. He wore a mark on his forehead, a ritual scar, to prove our noble blood.

He was a great man amongst our people but, to me, he was just my father. I remember his warm smile, and his

rich laughter when he played with me as a boy. I
remember sitting close to him, staring at the fire, as he
told stories of times long gone. He sat warm and near as
the night cooled. I felt safe with his powerful body by
my side. My heart lifted when his face smiled brightly
down at me.

We were a nation of dancers, musicians, and poets.
Every great event, such as a triumphant return from
battle, or a marriage, or a great harvest, was celebrated
with lavish dances, songs and music.

I still remember those drums and the voices rising
joyfully over me, making us one, sweeping us up
together in the great and ancient melodies of our people.
I remember hundreds of feet dancing, pounding the
warm, red earth.

Even now, I can see their robes, blue as the sky. Our
men and women all wore the same dress, a simple length
of calico, wrapped loosely about the body. The cloth was
dyed the deepest blue by a special berry that grew
abundantly in our valley. I have never seen such deep
blue fabric since, even in Europe.

I can still see my mother's blue robes sweeping around her body, and her golden bangles shining on her soft, brown arms that always caressed me so gently. She always wore a special perfume, made from flowers by the women in the village. Even today, whenever I smell certain flowers, I can almost see her.

Our valley was abundant. We had cattle, goats, chickens, yams, beans and corn. Each family had a garden, fenced with sticks. Nobody went hungry.

In the middle of our garden stood three thatched houses, supported by simple walls of wattle and clay.

We had three houses, and many rooms: Rooms for the day, rooms for eating, others for sleeping, and a special room for receiving guests, who would sit on perfumed benches.

Our slaves and their families slept in small shacks at the edge of our garden. As a small boy, I never imagined that I would one day become a slave myself.

Our farms were far from the village, so when we went farming we all went together with a hundred or more of us - men, women and children - would walk together through the forest to the great clearing where our farmland lay. We sang as we walked, carrying hoes, axes, picks and weapons too - in case of attack. Battles often took place near the great clearing, for many neighbouring peoples farmed there.

When we marched, we took guns, bows, double-edged swords and javelins. We had shields as tall as a man. All our people knew how to use weapons. Even our women were warriors. They often marched bravely out to fight along with the men. Our whole district was a kind of militia. Upon a certain signal, such as the firing of a gun at night, everyone would rise instantly, grab their weapons, and rush upon the enemy.

Most of our battles were fought with neighbouring peoples. Often these battles were fought for slaves. It was profitable to take prisoners and then either sell them back to their families or sell them to the traders who regularly passed through the valley.

Often, a chief would sell on his slaves to passing traders. Sometimes, he would even sell members of his own tribe as slaves. In this way, traders could get slaves merely by tempting chiefs and elders with fine goods. However, if they did not get what they wanted, they might try to take people by force.

We were enthusiastic in battle. Our men and women fought like lions. I remember, as a small boy, witnessing a battle that took place on our farmland in the great clearing.

We had been working all day harvesting our crops when suddenly we were attacked. I was still too small to wield a weapon, and so - as the attackers ran at us - my mother shouted at me to run away as fast as I could. I fled through the tall grass, until I reached the edge of the forest. I was breathless, and my heart pounded in my ears as the cries of battle echoed from across the field. Growing curious, although still trembling, I climbed a tall tree and watched the battle from a height.

Even from that distance, I could make out our people, for they all wore the blue cloth for which our valley was famous. Women, as well as men, fought on both sides. I watched with pride - and fear - as my mother slashed at the enemy with her broad sword. The fight was long and furious. From my perch in the tree, it seemed to last for hours. I groaned aloud each time I saw one of our people fall. I feared, above all, for my mother. After the battle was won, I rushed into her arms, and we both wept at the joy of seeing each other alive.

Although many of us were killed that day, we had won a great victory. We even took the enemy chief prisoner! He was carried off amid great songs of triumph. He offered us a large ransom for his life, but was put to death nonetheless.

In that battle, we also killed a famously beautiful virgin from the enemy tribe, and her arm was hung with pride in our marketplace, where trophies from hunts and battles were always displayed.

The spoils of battle were shared out according to who had fought hardest and had killed the greatest number of our enemy. The prisoners who were not sold on, or ransomed by their families, were kept as slaves by our people – but how different were their lives from the slaves in the West Indies! With us, they did the same amount of work as their masters and their food, clothing and lodging were nearly the same as ours. Some of our slaves were even allowed to have their own slaves, for their own use.

Yet there was more to us than war. We were also a spiritual people. My people believe in one creator of all things, and that he lives in the sun, and is girded with a belt so that he cannot eat or drink. However, according to some, he does smoke a pipe, which is also our own favourite luxury.

After death, it was believed that most souls are reincarnated in new-born babies, to begin life's cycle again. However, some may choose to stay in spirit form to protect us from evil spirits and enemies.

These protector spirits were usually deceased friends or relatives. Before each meal, we would always leave food on the ground for them, to sustain them in their task.

We did not forget our dead. Some days, I would go with my mother to the graves of our loved ones. I would watch quietly as she, with great reverence, poured animal blood on their graves, in offering and in remembrance.

I loved my mother with all my being. I was constantly with her - even when she made these mournful offerings at her own mother's tomb, where she would spend most of the night in lamentation while I watched on, in silent fear.

My grandmother's tomb was a small solitary thatched house in a graveyard near the forest. The loneliness of the place, the darkness of the night, and the ceremony of grieving, were naturally awful and gloomy. This sadness was made harrowing by my mother's howling lamentations, echoed by the sinister shrieks of the blackbirds that flock to places of death. For me, as a small boy, it was a scene of inexpressible terror.

Yet our simple religion was more about light than darkness. The sun's movements were of great importance, for it was the seat of God. When the sun would cross a certain line in the landscape, marking an equinox or a solstice, great rejoicing would begin. All across the land people made a great noise with rattles and held their hands up to heaven for a blessing.

Our wise men carefully watched the moon as well as the sun. At full moons near harvest, animals were slaughtered in sacrifice. The head of each family would kill an animal to bring luck to the whole household.

When women were having their monthly bleed, they were not allowed to touch anyone or any food. As I loved my mother so much, I could not keep from touching her. This meant that I too became impure and had to sleep with her in a special little cabin in the garden until we were both purified. In truth, I loved those times, when it was just the two of us, together in that little cabin.

We were a clean people, all the boys were circumcised and we held to many washing rituals - much like the ancient Jews. Indeed, some believe that we were descended from a branch of that great tribe.

In our appearance, we are much darker than the Jews, but perhaps this is because of our climate. It has been noticed that Spaniards who have been living a long while in South America often become dark-skinned.

If it is discovered that the complexions of the same people vary in different climates, it may help remove the prejudice that so many hold against the natives of Africa on account of our colour. Surely the minds of the Spaniards did not darken along with their complexions!

There are plenty of reasons to explain the current state of the African people. We should not try to limit the goodness of God, and imagine that he refused to give understanding to people made his own image, merely because they were carved in ebony.

Let the polished and haughty European remember that his ancestors were once, like the Africans, uncivilized, and even barbarous. Did Nature make them inferior to their sons? And should they too have been made slaves? Every rational mind answers, "no."

Let such thoughts melt the pride of those who imagine themselves superior. Let such pride be turned into sympathy for the wants and miseries of their dark-skinned brothers and sisters.

Understanding is not confined to people of any particular colour. God "made of one blood all nations of men" and"his wisdom is not our wisdom, nor are our ways his ways."

Chapter 2

Kidnapped

My memories of my country are but those of a child. For I was only eleven when I was taken from it.

Before I tell you how I was captured as a slave, let me tell you a little more about my family. There were seven of us children, six boys and one girl. My only sister and I were very close.

I was the youngest of the boys and so I became my mother's favourite. I spent every waking moment with her, and she took great pains to educate me. From an early age, I was trained in the arts of war, such as shooting and throwing the javelin. She adorned me with emblems, like those worn by brave warriors. My childhood life was a happy one, even though we lived with a constant fear of attackers and kidnappers.

To protect against kidnappers, when the grown-ups were out of the village, we children were often gathered in one place. One of us would be sent to climb up a tree, to keep lookout.

Once, I was keeping lookout up a tall tree when I saw some strange people coming to take the children gathered in my neighbour's garden. I let out a shout, and the older children managed to wrap one of the kidnappers in ropes, allowing time for some grown-ups to come to their aid.

However, on another occasion when time kidnappers came, we were not so lucky. One day, my sister and I were left to mind the house while the grown-ups were away working. Two men and a woman jumped over our walls, and in a flash, seized us both.

We had no time to fight back or to cry out, for they gagged our mouths, and ran off with us into the nearest wood. There they tied our hands, and carried us as far as they could. As night fell, we reached a small house, where the robbers stopped for food, and to spend the night.

We were untied but were unable to take any food, for we were overpowered by fatigue and grief. That first night, our only relief from our waking nightmare was a short and fitful sleep.

The next morning we left the house and travelled all day. Late in the day, we emerged from the woods and came into a road that I thought I knew. I hoped we might see someone who knew us. Or maybe my father might be there, waiting for us!

I saw some people at a distance and began to cry out for help, but the kidnappers just blocked my mouth, tied me tighter, and put me into a large sack. They also stopped my sister's mouth and tied her hands.

When we came to rest the following night they offered us some meat, but we could not eat - the only comfort we had was being in one another's arms. All that night, my sister and I bathed each other in our tears. But we were soon deprived of even the small comfort of weeping together.

The next day brought me a greater sorrow than I had ever known: my sister and I were separated. At first, we clung to each other so tightly that could not pull us apart. We begged them not to part us, but she was torn from me by the strong men, and was carried away.

I was left in a state of distraction that cannot be described. I cried and grieved continually for several days. I did not eat anything except what they forced into my mouth.

Eventually, after many days travelling, during which I was repeatedly bought and sold, I came into the hands of a chieftain, in a pleasant country. This man had two wives and some children, and all were kind to me. They did all they could to comfort me - particularly the chieftain's first wife, who reminded me of my mother.

Although I was a many days journey from my father's house, these people spoke exactly the same language as us. This first master of mine was a goldsmith. My main job was to work his bellows, which were of a type familiar from my home country. They were covered over with leather; and were worked like a pump to keep the fire hot. The molten gold that flowed was a beautiful bright yellow colour. From this, he made bracelets which the local women on their wrists and ankles.

I was there for about a month when they began to trust me to go a little distance from the house on my own. Of course, I took every opportunity to ask the way back to my own country.

To get my bearings, I went with the girls in the cool of the evenings, to bring jugs of water from the wells. I noted carefully where the sun rose in the morning, and where it set in the evening. I knew my father's house was towards the rising of the sun.

I was determined to seize the first opportunity I could to escape, for I was weighed down by grief after my mother and friends. I was ashamed too for, as a slave, I could not eat with the free-born children, even though I played with them often.

While I was planning my escape, one day an unlucky thing happened which threw my plans askew, and put an end to my hopes of seeing my father's house again.

I sometimes helped an elderly woman slave to cook and take care of the poultry. One morning, while I was feeding the chickens, and while throwing grain to them, I accidentally tossed a small pebble at one of them, which hit the bird on the head and immediately killed it.

The old slave woman soon missed the chicken and inquired after it. I told her the truth, for my mother told me never to tell a lie. But she flew into a violent rage and said that I would suffer for what I had done.

She ran to tell her mistress that I had killed a chicken and I expected an instant flogging, which to me was a dreadful thought, for I had seldom been beaten at home. I decided to run. I fled to a nearby thicket and hid deep it its leaves.

Soon afterwards my mistress came. When they couldn't

find me, they assumed I had run away, and so the whole neighbourhood was raised in my pursuit. In that part of the country, the houses and villages were skirted with woods and thick shrubs so thick and full of hiding places.

The neighbours spent the whole day looking for me, and several times came within a few yards of the place where I lay hidden. Every time I heard a rustling among the trees, I expected to be found out, and punished by my master: but they never discovered me, though they were often so near that I could hear them speaking.

I heard them say: "The boy must have fled towards home." But another said that the distance was so great, and the way so intricate, that I could never reach it, and that I would certainly end up lost or dead in the woods. When I heard this said, I was seized with a violent panic. My heart thumped in my chest and I began to despair.

Night began to fall, and my fears grew worse. I had entertained hopes of getting home, and I had planned to do so in the dark. But now, I was convinced it could not be done. I began to think that, even if I could escape the wild animals of the forests, I could not escape the humankind. As I lay there in the dark, despairing, wondering what to do, I felt like a hunted deer: Every leaf whispered death.

I heard rustlings among the leaves. I was sure they were snakes and, every moment, I expected to be bitten by them. This increased my anguish, and the horror of my situation became too much. I stumbled out of the thicket, faint and hungry, for I had not eaten or drunk a thing all day.

I crept back to my master's kitchen, from which I had run that morning. I lay down in the ashes of the fireplace and wished for death to come, to relieve me of all my pains.

I was half asleep the next morning when the old woman slave, who was always the first up, came to light the fire and saw me in the fireplace. She could scarcely believe her eyes. She now felt for me and promised to put in a good word with the master for me, as she went to fetch him. The master came, his face stern but kind. He scolded me only gently and ordered me to be taken care of.

Soon after my near-escape, I was again sold. I was now carried to the left of the sun's rising, through many different countries, and many great forests.

The journey was long, and I was small. When I grew tired, the people I was sold to carried me on their shoulders or on their backs. We passed many strong sheds along the way, built to accommodate the merchants and travellers on the road. They lay in those buildings at night, always well-armed.

From the time I left my own country I had always found somebody that understood me - until I came to the sea. The languages of those different nations I passed through did not totally differ from my own. Thus, while I was journeying through Africa, I learned two or three different tongues.

I had been travelling with these merchants for a considerable time when, one evening, to my great surprise, who did I see brought to the house where I was staying, but my dear sister!

As soon as she saw me she gave a loud shriek, and ran into my arms—I was overpowered by emotion, and neither of us could speak. Instead, we clung to each other in mutual embraces for a long time, unable to do anything but weep.

Our meeting affected all who saw us. I must admit that, although these masters deprived me of my freedom, they did not mistreat me, or any other of their slaves - except to tie us up, when necessary, to keep us from running away.

When these people realised that we were brother and sister, they gave us time together. My sister and I held one another by the hands all night and, for a while, we forgot our misfortunes in the joy of being together. Yet this brief happiness was soon to end. Dawn proved fatal to it, for scarcely had morning come when she was once again torn from me.

I was now more miserable, if possible, than before. Her presence had given me some small relief from my pain. This disappeared with her. My sister's absence left a vast void in my heart. My worries for her were doubled. I knew how much she was suffering, and I knew that I couldn't help her.

I would have given my life to get her free. In the night, I would re-live happy times from our childhood in my mind.

She is today still riveted to my heart, and nothing will ever remove her image from my mind. I have come to know a God who protects the weak from the strong. I ask him to protect her, though I know that she may already be with him. For she may long ago have fallen victim to the violence of the African trader, the sick stench of a slave ship, or the lash and lust of a brutal and unrelenting overseer.

Not long after my sister was taken from me a second time, I was again sold, and carried through a number of places. After travelling for many weeks, I came to a town called Tinmah, in the most beautiful country I have ever seen in Africa.

It was extremely fertile and lush, and many small streams flowed through its streets, before meeting at a large pond in the centre of the town, where people washed.

The town had broad leafy trees, which gave wide shady spaces between the neat, whitewashed houses. Here I first saw and tasted coconuts, which I thought the most delicious things I had ever tasted. Here I also tasted sugar cane for the first time.

Their money consisted of little white shells, the size of a fingernail. I was sold here for one hundred and seventy-two of these shells by a merchant. After two or three days at his house, a wealthy widow neighbour of his visited one evening. She brought with her an only son, a young lad about my own age and size. They saw me and, having taken a fancy to me, they bought me and went home with them.

Her house and lands and were the finest I ever saw in Africa. She had several slaves to attend her. The next day I was washed and perfumed and, when mealtime came, I was asked to sit and eat with my mistress and her son.

I was astonished! How could they let me, who was a bound slave, to eat with they who were free? Soon, all their kind treatment of me made me forget that I was a slave.

The language of these people resembled ours so closely, that we understood each other perfectly. They had also the very same customs as my people. There were likewise slaves daily to attend me, while my young master and I with other boys sported with our darts and bows and arrows, as I used to do at home.

After two months of such happiness, I began to think I was to be adopted into the family. By degrees, I began to forget my misfortunes, when all at once the delusion vanished. Without warning, early one morning, I was woken from my dreams and taken, this time to a place worse than before. This brief taste of joy was to make its opposite all more bitter.

Soon I was to see the sea: an element I had never before beheld, and which had no idea even existed. Upon it, I found hardship and unending cruelty which I can only remember with utter horror.

Until now, the nations and people I had encountered resembled my own in their manners, customs, and language. But now I came upon a place where the inhabitants differed from us in all possible ways.

I was very much struck by these differences. These people did not circumcise and ate without washing their hands. They cooked also in iron pots and had European swords and crossbows, which were unknown to my people. They often had fistfights amongst themselves. Their women were not so modest as ours, for they ate, drank, and slept with their men.

Above all, I was amazed to see no sacrifices or offerings to God take place among them. These terrifying people decorated themselves with scars and filed their teeth very sharp. They sometimes tried to decorate me with scars and to sharpen my teeth, but I would not allow them. I hoped I wouldn't be among them too long.

At last, I came to the banks of a large river, which was covered with canoes. The people there seemed to live in these canoes, with their household utensils and provisions of all kinds. I was astonished at this, as I had never before seen any water larger than a pond or a stream. My surprise was mingled with fear when I was put into one of these canoes, and we began to paddle along the river.

We continued moving along the river until nightfall. When we landed, we made fires on the riverbanks, each family by themselves. Some dragged their canoes ashore, while others stayed and cooked in theirs afloat, and laid in them all night. Those on the land had mats, out of which they made tents. Some in the shape of little houses. We slept in one of these and, after the morning meal, we embarked again and proceeded down the river as before. I was astonished to see some of the women, as well as the men, jump into the water, dive to the bottom, come up again and swim about with ease.

For six or seven months after I was kidnapped, I continued to travel, sometimes by land and water, through different countries, until I eventually arrived at the sea.

The first thing that greeted my eyes when I arrived at the coast was a slave ship, riding at anchor, waiting for its cargo. The immense blue sea and the huge and complex ship upon it filled me with astonishment. However, this was soon converted into terror when I was carried on board.

I was immediately manhandled and tossed about by the crew, to see if I were strong, and of any value. I was convinced that I had gotten into a world of evil spirits, and that they were going to kill me. This idea seemed proven to me by their pale skin and their strange language. Such was my horror, that if I had owned ten thousand worlds, I would have freely parted with them at that moment, all to become the lowest slave in my own country.

Looking around the ship, I saw a large furnace and a multitude of black people of every description chained together, every one of their faces expressing dejection and sorrow.

I was no longer doubtful of my fate. Overpowered with anguish, I fell motionless on the deck and fainted. When I recovered a little, I found some black people around me, who talked to me in order to cheer me, but in vain.

I asked them if we were soon to be eaten by those white men with horrible looks, red faces, and loose hair. They told me I was not. One of the crew brought me a small portion of liquor in a wine glass but - being afraid of him - I would not take it out of his hand. One of the blacks, therefore, took it from him and gave it to me, and I swallowed a little. However, instead of reviving me, this threw me into consternation at the strange feeling it produced, for I had never tasted liquor before.

Soon after this, the blacks who brought me on board went away and left me abandoned to despair. I then knew I had no chance of returning to my native country. I even wished for my former slavery instead of that horror-filled ship.

I had little time to indulge my grief. I was soon put down below decks, where my nostrils met a stench, unlike anything I had experienced before. The loathsomeness of the stink, and the crying all about me, made me so sick and low that I was unable to eat.

I now saw death as my last friend in the world. I begged death to come and relieve me. Before long, two of the white men offered me food. When I refused to eat, one of them tied me down across the windlass, while the other flogged me severely.

I had never experienced anything like this before. Although I feared the sea, if I could have got over the nettings, I would have jumped over the side.

But the nettings were too high, and the crew used to watch us very closely when we were not chained down to the decks, in case we should leap into the water. I saw some of these poor African prisoners severely cut for attempting to do so and whipped hourly for not eating.

I found some of my own nation amongst the poor, chained men. Meeting them eased to my mind, to a small degree. I asked them what would happen to us. They told me we would be carried to the white people's country to work for them. I then was a little cheered, and thought, if it were no worse than working, things were not so desperate.

However, I still feared I would be put to death. These white people looked fearful and acted in savage a manner. I had never seen so many instances of brutal cruelty - and not only towards us blacks, but also to some of the whites themselves.

I saw one particular white man flogged so unmercifully with a large rope near the foremast, that he died as a result. They just tossed him over the side as they would a dead animal. This made me fear these people the more. I expected to be treated the same way. I could not help expressing my fears and to my countrymen. I asked if these people had no country but instead lived in this "hollow place," as we called the ship.

I asked my countrymen, "how come none of us have ever heard of these white men?" They said it was because they came from so very far away. I asked where the white women were. I was told that they had women, but they'd left them behind.

I asked how the vessel could go. They told me they did not know, but that there were cloths put upon the masts by the ropes, and then the vessel went, perhaps by magic. They said the white men also had some spell or magic they put in the water to stop the vessel. I was amazed at this and now was more certain than ever that the white men were spirits.

I expected they would sacrifice me and I would have done anything to escape. But it was impossible for any of us to make our escape.

While we stayed on the coast, I was mostly on deck during the daytime. One day, to my great astonishment, I saw another one of these vessels coming in with its white sails up. As soon as the white men saw it, they gave a great shout, at which we were amazed.

The vessel became larger as it came nearer. At last, she came to an anchor in my sight, and when the anchor was let go I and my countrymen were lost in astonishment to observe the vessel stop, but we were no longer convinced it was done by magic.

The white men from the other ship then launched their small boats and came on board our ship. The people of both ships seemed very glad to see each other. Several of the strangers also shook hands with us black people, and made motions with their hands, signifying that we were to go to their country, but we did not understand them.

At last, when our ship had taken on board all her cargo, the sailors made ready with fearful noises. We were all put below decks so that we could not see how they managed the vessel. But this disappointment was the least of my sorrow. The stench of the hold, while we were on the coast, was so intolerably bad, that it was dangerous to remain there for any time. Before we set sail, some of us had been allowed to stay on the deck for fresh air. Now that the whole ship's cargo was confined below together, it became absolutely pestilential in the heat of that climate.

The hold was so crowded that each person chained lying down scarcely had room to turn themselves over. We almost suffocated. We sweated in the heat, and the air soon became unfit to breathe. This brought on a sickness among the slaves, and many died.

The people were in agony from the constant chafing of their chains. The toilet tubs were full of filth, into which the small children often fell, and almost drowned.

The shrieks of the women, and the groans of the dying, rendered it a scene of inconceivable horror. Perhaps luckily for me, I soon became so sick that the white men thought it better to keep me on deck most of the time.

Because I was only a boy of twelve, I was not put in chains. I thought I would die, like so many of my companions, who were daily brought upon deck at the point of death. I began to hope that death would soon put an end to my miseries.

I thought the strange creatures that lived in the deep sea, were much luckier than me. I envied them their freedom. I wished I could become one of them.

As the days went by, my pain and constant fear increased. The more I saw of these white men, the crueller I found them to be. One day, they had caught a great number of fish, but when they had killed and eaten as many as they wanted, they just tossed the remaining fish into the sea again - even though we begged and pleaded for some to eat.

If any of the slaves even tried to take a pinch of their fish scraps, they got severe floggings. One day, in mid-ocean, when we had a smooth sea and moderate wind, two of my wearied countrymen were chained together near me. I looked up, to see them rushing at the nettings which fenced the side of the ship. Somehow, they made it through. Another very sick man glanced up, saw them, and rushed in behind them. Many others would have followed them, except the crew stopped them. Many of us would have preferred death over the misery we were experiencing on that ship.

After they jumped, noise and confusion broke out amongst the crew. They stopped the ship and turned about to get the slaves. However, two of the wretches were drowned, but they got the other. Afterwards, they flogged him unmercifully for preferring death to slavery.

Throughout this long voyage, we underwent more hardships than I can tell you about. Often, we were near suffocation from the lack of fresh air. This, and the stench from the toilet tubs, carried many off.

During our passage, I saw flying fishes for the first time, which surprised me greatly. They often flew across the ship, and many of them fell upon the deck.

I also saw a sextant being used for the first time. I was often curious to see the sailors make observations with it, but I could not think what this meant. They eventually took notice of my amazement and one of them, willing to indulge my curiosity, let me look through it.

Through the telescope, the clouds appeared to be as solid as land. This heightened my wonder and I became more sure than ever that I was in another world, and that everything about me was magic.

At last, we came within sight of the island of Barbados. When it appeared, the whites on board gave a great shout, and made many signs of joy to us. We did not know what to think of this but, as the vessel drew nearer land, we saw the harbour, and other ships of different kinds and sizes. Soon, we anchored amongst them off Bridge Town.

Many merchants and planters now came on board, although it was evening. They put us in separate groups and examined us attentively. They also made us jump, and pointed to the land, signifying we were to go there. We thought this meant we would be eaten by these ugly men, as they seemed to us. Soon after, we were all put down below decks again. There was much dread and trembling among us. Nothing but bitter cries were heard all that night.

The cries were so bad that the white people got some old slaves from the land to come and pacify us. They told us we were not to be eaten, but we were to work. They said we were soon to go on to the land, where we would see many of our country people. This news eased our minds. Sure enough, soon after we were landed, Africans of all languages came to greet us.

We were brought immediately to the merchant's yard, where we were all pent up together like sheep in a fold, without regard to our sex or age. As everything was new to me, all that I saw filled me with surprise.

What struck me first was that the houses were built in stories, one on top of the other. They were different from African houses in many ways. But I was most astonished of all to see people on horseback. I did not know what this could mean. I thought these people were full of nothing but magical arts.

While I was in this state of amazement, one of my fellow prisoners spoke to another about the horses. He said they were the same kind as they had in their country. I understood their speech, even though they were from a distant part of Africa. Afterwards, when I came to converse with different Africans, I found they had many horses amongst them in other parts of Africa, even though but I had never seen one before.

After a few days in the merchant's custody, we were sold. They had a strange way of conducting their sales. Once a signal was given, such as the beating of a drum, the buyers rushed into the yard where the slaves were held and chose the parcel they liked best.

The noise and clamour involved in all this, and the eager, greedy faces of the buyers, served to increase the fears of the terrified Africans. We believed that the buyers were the bringers of our inevitable doom. During these auctions - without thought - relations and friends were separated, and most would never see each other again.

In the ship in which I was brought over, in the men's section, there were several brothers, who were sold in different lots in the sale. It was very moving to see and hear their sorrowful cries when they parted.

Yet they call themselves Christians! Might not an African ask them, did you learn this from your God, who says unto you, "Do unto others as you would have them do unto you"?

Is it not enough that we are torn from our country, and our friends, to toil for your luxury and lust for fain? Must every tender feeling be sacrificed to your greed? Are the closest friends and relations to be parted from each other, and prevented from cheering the gloom of slavery with the small comfort of being together, and sharing their sufferings and sorrows?

Why are parents to lose their children, brothers their sisters, or husbands their wives? Surely this is a new refinement in cruelty. For it gives no advantage for the slavers, but only adds distress, and fresh horror, even to the wretchedness of slavery.

CHAPTER 3

VIRGINIA

.

I now the small remnants of comfort I had enjoyed. No longer could I speak with my countrymen, for they were gone. The women who used to wash me, and take care of me, were also now gone to different places. I never saw them again.

I was kept on the island of Barbados for a number of days. Within a fortnight, myself and some other slaves - who unsellable because we were crying too much - were shipped off for North America in a small ship. In this passage, we were treated better than when we were coming from Africa. We had plenty rice and fat pork to eat. We landed up a river a good way in from the sea, near Virginia county. In this new land, we saw few if any of our fellow Africans. There was not one soul who could talk to me.

Soon, all my companions from the ship were sent different ways, and I was left alone. I was brought to a plantation, and put to work weeding grass and gathering stones. I became unbearably miserable. I thought myself worse off than any of the rest of my companions from the ship, for at least they could talk to each other. I had no person to speak to that I could understand.

I was constantly grieving and pining. I wished for death rather than anything else. While I was on this plantation, the man who owned the estate became unwell. One day, I was sent to his house to fan him. I was terrified by some things I saw. As I came through the house I saw a black woman slave, who was cooking the dinner. The poor creature was cruelly loaded with various kinds of iron devices. She had one iron contraption on her head, which locked her mouth closed, so that she could scarcely speak and could not eat nor drink.

I was shocked at this cruel device, which I later learned was called the iron muzzle. A fan was put into my hand, to fan the man while he slept, which work I did with great fear. While he was fast asleep, I had time to look about the room, which appeared both very fine and strange.

The first thing which I noticed was a watch which hung on the chimney. I was surprised by the ticking noise it made, and I was afraid it would tell the gentleman if I did anything wrong. I also saw a picture hanging in the room, which appeared constantly to look at me. I was terrified by this, having never seen such a thing before.

I thought it was something magical. Because it did not move, I thought it might be some strange way the white people had to keep important people after they died. I wondered if they offered them food and drink, as we used to do to our friendly spirits. I remained in this state of fear until my master awoke when I was dismissed from the room. I was relieved to leave, for I thought these people were full of strange wonders.

In the plantation, I was called Jacob. However, on board the ship I had been called Michael. I was some time in this miserable, forlorn and dejected state, with nobody to talk to, when the kind hand of God brought me comfort. One day, the captain of a merchant ship, called the Industrious Bee, came to my master's house on business. This gentleman's name was Michael Henry Pascal. He had been a lieutenant in the Royal Navy, but he now commanded a trading ship.

While he was at my master's house he saw me and liked me so well that he bought me for thirty or forty pounds sterling. He intended to give me as a present to some friends of his in England. An elderly black man brought where the ship lay on horseback. I found this way of travelling very odd. I was carried on board this fine large ship, which was ready to sail for England, loaded with tobacco and other cargo.

I now felt that my situation had much improved. I had sails to lie on, and plenty of good food to eat. Everyone on board treated me very kindly, unlike what I had seen of white people before. I, therefore, began to think that the white people were not all the same.

A few days later, we sailed for England. I still had no idea where I was going, or what would happen. By this time, however, I could speak a smattering of imperfect English. I wanted to know where we were going. Some of the people of the ship told me they were going to bring me back to my own country, which made me very happy. I rejoiced at the idea of going back. I imagined myself at home telling my people of wonders I had seen. But I was destined for another fate.

When we came within sight of the English coast, I knew I had been deceived. While I was on board this ship, my master named me Gustavus Vassa. I began to understand him a little, and refused to be called this name. I told him that I would be called Jacob, but he said I should not, and still called me Gustavus. When, at first, I refused to answer to my new name, he hit me. In the end, I gave in and began to bear this name, by which I have been known by ever since.

The voyage across the Atlantic took longer than expected, and we began to run short of provisions. In the end, we had a pound and a half of bread each per week, and about the same amount of meat. We were only allowed two pints of water a day.

We only met with one other ship the whole time we were at sea. Only once did we catch a few fish. When we ran low on food, the captain and people thought it was funny to tell me that they would kill and eat me. I thought they were serious, and I became depressed beyond measure. I expected every moment to be my last.

One evening they caught a large shark and got it on board with a great deal of trouble. This gladdened my poor heart, as I thought they would eat it instead of me. Yet to my astonishment, they just cut off a small part of its tail, and tossed the rest over the side. This renewed my worries. I did not know what to think of these white people. I very much feared they would kill and eat me.

There was a young lad on board the ship who had never been at sea before. He was about four or five years older than me. His name was Richard Baker and he was an American. He had received an excellent education and was friendly and kind to me. As soon as I came on board he showed me a great deal of kindness and attention. I grew extremely fond of him. We soon became inseparable. For the following two years, he was to help me in many ways and became my constant companion, and my teacher.

Although this kind young fellow had many slaves of his own, Richard I went through many sufferings together on board the ship. We spent many nights close together, when we were in great distress. A friendship was cemented between us which we both cherished until his death, which, to my sorrow, came too early. He died in, 1759, when he was up the Archipelago, on board his majesty's ship the Preston. I lost a kind companion and a faithful friend. I lost someone who, at the age of just fifteen, had a mind superior to prejudice. He was never ashamed to be the friend and teacher to someone who was ignorant, a stranger, of a different complexion, and a slave.

My master had stayed in Richard's mother's house in America. He respected him very much, always ate with him in the cabin. He often used to joke to Richard that he would kill me to eat. Sometimes he would say to me that the black people were not good to eat, and would ask me if we did not eat people in my country. I said, no. Then he said he would kill Dick first, and me afterwards.

Though this relieved my mind little as to the danger I was in, I became alarmed for Dick. Whenever he was called for, I used to be terrified he was about to be killed. I would anxiously peep in to see if they were going to kill him. I was not free from this terrible anxiety until we made landfall.

One night, we lost a man overboard. I was below and did not know what had happened. The sudden cries and noise were so great that, as usual, I became terrified. I believed that they were about to make an offering of me, and to perform some magic - which I still believed they dealt in.

As the waves were very high I thought the God which ruled the seas was angry, and so I expected to be offered up to appease him. This filled my mind with agony. I lay awake all night in anxious terror. However, when daylight appeared I became a little eased in my mind. Every time I was called, I thought that I was being brought to be killed.

Sometime after this, we saw some very large fish, which I later learned were called grampuses. They appeared at dusk and looked extremely strange in the twilight. They were so close that they blew water on the ship's deck. I believed them to be the rulers of the sea. As the white people did not make offerings, I felt sure that these rulers of the sea would be angry with them. My belief seemed confirmed when the wind just then died away. A calm ensued, and the ship stopped going. I was sure that the strange fish had done this. I hid myself in the forward part of the ship, in fear of being offered up to appease them. I was every minute watching and quaking, but my good friend Dick soon came to comfort me. I asked him, as best I could, what these fish were.

Since I spoke little English, I only barely made him understand my question. He did not understand my meaning at all when I asked him if offerings would be made to them. However, he did tell me these fish would swallow anybody, which alarmed me.

He was then called away by the captain, who was leaning over the quarter-deck railing, looking at the fish. The crew were busy getting a barrel of pitch to light. The captain now called me, having learned of my fears from Dick. The captain and crew amused themselves with my fears, since my crying and trembling seemed ludicrous to them. They continued laughing at me for a time, before dismissing me. The barrel of pitch was then lit and thrown over the side into the water. By this time, it was just dark, and the fish went after it and, to my great joy, I saw them no more.

All my fears began to subside when we came in sight of land. At last, the ship arrived at Falmouth in England, after a voyage of thirteen weeks. Every heart on board was gladdened to reach the shore, but none more so than mine.

The captain immediately went ashore, and sent fresh provisions on board, which we badly needed. We made good use of them, and our famine suddenly turned into feasting, almost without ending.

I arrived in England in the spring of 1757. I was almost twelve years of age at that time. I was very much struck by the buildings and paved streets of Falmouth. Indeed, any object I saw filled me with fresh surprise. One morning, when I went on deck, I found it covered with snow, which had fallen overnight I had never seen anything like this before, so I thought it was salt.

I immediately ran down to the mate and asked him to come and see how somebody had thrown salt all over the deck in the night. He, knowing what it was, told me to bring some of it down to him. I ran back with a handful of it, which I found very cold indeed. When I brought it to him, he asked me to taste it. I did so, and I was surprised beyond measure. I then asked him what it was. He told me it was snow, but I could not understand what he meant. He asked me if we had such a thing in my country and I told him, no. I then asked him what it was for, and who made it. He told me a great man in the heavens, called God. Here again, I was at a loss to understand him, all the more so, I soon saw the air filled with it, as a heavy snow shower began to fall.

After this I went to ashore to church and, having never been at such a place before, I was amazed at seeing and hearing the service. I asked all I could about it. They told me that this was the worship of God, who made us and all things. I soon got into an endless field of questions, insofar as I was able to ask about things.

My young friend Dick was the best at explaining things to me, for I could speak freely with him. He enjoyed teaching me and, from what I could understand from him about this God - and seeing these white people did not sell one another, as we did - I was very pleased. In this respect, I thought they were happier than we Africans.

I was astonished at the wisdom of the white people in all the things I saw. I was amazed that they did not offer sacrifices, or make any offerings, or eat with unwashed hands. I could not help noticing the particular slenderness of their women, which I did not like at first. I thought they were not as modest and demure as the African women.

I often saw my master and Dick engrossed in their reading. I had a great curiosity to talk to the books, as I thought they did. For I wanted to learn the origins of things. For that purpose, when alone, I often took up a book, talked to it, and then put my ears to it, hoping that it would answer me. I was very concerned when it remained silent.

My master lodged at the house of a gentleman in Falmouth, who had a fine little daughter about six or seven years of age who grew very fond of me. We even used to eat together and had the servants wait on us. I was so well looked after by this family that it often reminded me of the treatment I had received from my little noble African master.

After a few happy days in Falmouth, I was sent back on board the ship. But the child cried after me so much that nothing could pacify, so I was sent for again. I began to fear I would be married to this young lady, when my master asked me if I would stay there with her as he was going away with the ship, which had taken tobacco on board. I cried and said that I would not leave her. In the end, they sneaked me back on board the ship again. We then sailed for the island of Guernsey, which was not far away. This was where one of the ship's owners lived. He was a merchant named Nicholas Doberry.

As I was now amongst a people who did not have their faces scarred, like some of the African nations where I had been, I was very glad I had not let them decorate me in that way when I was with them.

When we arrived at Guernsey, my master sent me to stay with one of his mates, who had a wife and family there.

Some months later, he went to England, and left me in care of this mate, along with my friend Dick.

This mate also had a little daughter called Mary, aged about five or six years, whom I loved to play with. I often noticed that when her mother washed her face it looked very rosy; but when she washed mine it did not look so. I therefore often tried to see if I could wash my face so it became of the same colour as my little play-mate's, but it was no use. I began to be mortified at the difference in our complexions. Mary's mother treated me with great kindness, taught me everything and treated me just the same as her own child.

I stayed there until the summer of 1757. That summer, my master sent for me, Dick and his old mate with news that he had been made first lieutenant of his majesty's naval ship, the Roebuck. We all then left Guernsey, and set out for England in a sloop bound for London.

As we were coming up towards the Nore, where the Roebuck lay, a man of war's boat came alongside to find men and boys on board to be pressed into the navy. When they came alongside, every man ran to hide himself. I was very much frightened by this, though I did not know what it meant, or what to think or do. However I went and hid myself also under a hencoop. Moments later, the press-gang came on board with their swords drawn, and searched all about, pulling people out by force, and putting them into the boat.

In the end, I was found too. The man who found me held me up by my heels while they all made sport of me. I roared and cried out all the time until, at last, my master's mate came to my assistance. He did all he could to pacify me, but nothing could calm me until I saw the press gang's boat sail away from us.

Soon afterwards, we came to the Nore, where the Roebuck lay. To our great joy, my master came on board, and brought us to the great ship. When I went on board this large ship, I was amazed to see the quantity of men and the huge guns. However, my surprise began to diminish as my knowledge increased. I no longer felt the terrors which had taken hold of me when I first came amongst Europeans. I even began to pass towards the opposite extreme. Far from being afraid of everything new that I saw, after some time in this ship, I even began to long for battle.

Grief doesn't last forever in young minds, and my grief began to wear away. I soon began to enjoy myself pretty well, and to feel easy aboard the warship. There was a number of boys on aboard, which still made it all the more enjoyable. We were always together, and spent a great part of our time playing.

I stayed on this ship for a long time. We went on several voyages and visited many places. We went to Holland twice and brought important people back to England from there. One day, when we were at sea, all the boys were called on the quarter-deck. For the amusement of the gentlemen, we were paired and made to fight. For this, the gentleman gave us from five to nine shillings each.

That was the first time I had ever fought with a white boy. I had never known what it was to have a bloody nose before. This strange sensation made me fight desperately. My fight went on for more than an hour. At last, when both of us were weary, we were parted. I had a great deal of this kind of sport afterwards. The captain and the ship's crew used to encourage me to fight.

Another time, the ship went to Leith in Scotland. We sailed from there to the Orkney islands, where I was surprised to see scarcely any night. From there, we sailed in company with a great fleet, full of soldiers, bound for England.

During all this time, our ship had never gone into battle with an enemy ship, even though we often cruised off the coast of France, which was at war with England. We did chase many ships, and captured seventeen as prizes, but each without a fight.

I learned many of the manoeuvres of the ship during our cruise and I had to fire the guns several times. One evening, off Havre de Grace, just as it was growing dark, we met with a fine, large French frigate. We immediately got everything ready for fighting. I expected that I should, at last, see the engagement which I had so long wished for. But just as the command was given to fire, we heard those on board the other ship cry "Haul down the jib". In that instant, she hoisted English colours. There was instantly with us a cry of "Avast! stop firing!". I think one or two guns had been let off, but luckily they did no harm. We had hailed the French-built ship several times; but as they hadn't heard us, we received no answer and took her for an enemy ship. She proved to be the Ambuscade man of war, to my great disappointment.

We returned to Portsmouth, without having been in any action, just at the trial of Admiral Byng - whom I saw several times during the case. As my master had left the ship, and gone to London for promotion, Dick and I were put on board the "man of war" – which was the term for warship – named Savage, to help refloat another navy ship that had run aground on the coast. After a few weeks on board the Savage, Dick and I were sent on shore at Deal, where we remained for a short time.

My master sent for us to come to London, a place I had long wished to see. We were delighted to travel by waggon to London, where we stayed with Mr. Guerin, a relative of my master. This gentleman had two sisters. They were very amiable ladies, who took great care of me.

Although I had longed to see London, when I arrived I was unfortunately unable to satisfy my curiosity. I became so ill that I could not stand for several months, and had to be sent to St. George's Hospital. In the hospital, I grew so ill, that the doctors even wanted to cut my left leg off at various times, fearing that it would become gangrenous. But I always said I would rather die than allow my leg to be cut of, and happily I recovered without the operation.

Just as I recovered from the chilblains, small-pox broke out on me, so that I was again confined to bed. I thought myself particularly unlucky. However, I soon recovered again. By this time, my master had been promoted to first lieutenant of the Preston – new a man of war of fifty guns, then lying at Deptford. Dick and I were sent aboard her and we soon sailed to Holland to bring over a Duke to England.

While I was aboard this ship an incident happened, which - though small - it struck me at the time, as I considered it the work of God. One morning, a young man was looking up to the fore-top, and the language common on ships, he "damned his eyes", about something. Just at that moment, some small particles of dirt fell into his left eye and by that evening, it was very much inflamed. The next day it grew worse; and within six or seven days he lost his eye.

From this ship, my master was appointed a lieutenant on board the Royal George. When he was going, he wished me to stay on board the Preston, to learn the French horn. But the ship being ordered for Turkey, I could not think of leaving my master, as I was very warmly attached to him. I told him that if he left me behind, it would break my heart. This helped persuade him to take me with him. But he left Dick on board the Preston, I embraced him when we parted, for the last time.

The Royal George was the largest ship I had ever seen. When I came aboard her, I was surprised at the large number of people. There were men, women and children, of every sort. I was amazed at the huge size of the guns, many of which were made of brass, which was something I had never seen before.

On board, there were shops or stalls for every kind of goods. The sellers were calling out as in a market in a town. To me, the ship seemed like a little world, into which I was again cast without a friend, for I had no longer my dear companion Dick.

We did not stay long here. My master was not many weeks on board before he got an appointment to become the sixth lieutenant of the Namur, which was then at Spithead. The Namur was fitting up to come under the command of Vice-admiral Boscawen, who was to sail with a large fleet against Louisburgh.

The entire crew of the Royal George were turned over to the Namur, and the flag of the gallant admiral was hoisted on board, the blue at the maintop-gallant masthead. There was a great fleet of men of war of every sort assembled together for this expedition. I was hoping to soon have the chance to be in a real sea-fight.

Our mighty fleet combined with Admiral Cornish's fleet, which was destined for the East Indies. Once all was ready, we at last weighed anchor and set sail. The two fleets continued in company for several days, and then parted. Before the fleets separated, Admiral Cornish in the Lenox first saluted our admiral in the Namur with a volley of canon fire, which booming salute was returned.

We then steered for America, but contrary winds drove us to Tenerife. I was struck by the famous mountainous peak of this island. Its enormous height, and its sugar-loaf shape, filled me with wonder.

We remained in sight of this island for some days, before we proceeded to America, where we soon arrived. We sailed into a large harbour called St. George, in Halifax. Here, we had plenty fish and fresh food to eat. While we waited in the bay, we were joined by different men of war and transport ships with soldiers. Soon, our fleet comprised a great number of ships of all kinds. Our newly enlarged fleet then sailed for Cape Breton in Nova Scotia.

We had the gallant General Wolfe on board our ship, whose friendly nature made him beloved by all the men. He often honoured me, and other boys, with attention. He even saved me from a flogging once, for fighting with a young gentleman.

We arrived at Cape Breton in the summer of 1758. All the soldiers landed, in order to make an attack upon Louisbourgh. My master oversaw the landing, and I saw a battle erupt between our men and the enemy. The French waiting on the shore to attack us, and they disrupted our landing for a long time, but they were eventually driven from their trenches and the landing was a success.

Our troops pursued the French as far as the town of Louisburgh. In this battle, many were killed on both sides.

I saw a strange thing that day: a lieutenant of the Princess Amelia, was giving a word of command and, while his mouth was open, a musket ball went through it and passed out through his cheek. I had that day in my hand the scalp of an Indian king, who was killed in the engagement. The scalp had been taken off by an Highlander. I saw this king's ornaments too, which were strange, and made of feathers.

Our land forces laid siege to the town of Louisbourgh, while our fleet kept the French ships blocked up in the harbour. At the same time, batteries of cannon fired upon the trapped French ships from the land. They fired with such effect, that one day I saw some of the French ships set on fire.

Another time, about fifty boats belonging to the English men of war attacked and boarded the only two remaining French men of war in the harbour. They also set fire to a seventy-gun ship, but they captured a sixty-four gun ship, called the Bienfaisant. During my stay I had often the opportunity of being near Captain Balfour, who kind to me, and liked me so much that he often asked my master to let him have me. Yet my master would not part with me, and no payment could have induced me to leave him.

At last, Louisbourgh was taken, and the English men of war came into the town's harbour, to my very great joy. I had now the liberty to indulge myself ashore, where I went often. When the ships were in the harbour, we had the most beautiful water-borne procession that I ever saw. All the admirals and captains of the men of war, full dressed, and in their barges, ornamented with pendants, came alongside of the Namur.

The vice-admiral then went on shore in his barge, followed by the other officers in order of seniority, to take possession of the town and fort. A while after this, the French governor and his lady, and other persons of note, came on board our ship to dine. Our ships were dressed with colourful flags, from the mast head to the deck. This, together with the firing of our guns, made a magnificent spectacle.

As soon as everything was settled, we sailed with part of the fleet for England, leaving some ships behind in Louisbourgh. It was now winter. During our passage home, when we were approaching the English channel and beginning to look for land, we saw the sails of seven large men of war. Many people on board our ship said that these must be English men of war. Some of the crew even began to name some of the ships. By this time that the two fleets began to mingle, and our admiral ordered his flag to be hoisted.

Just then, the other fleet hoisted their French ensigns, and shot a broadside of cannon at us as they passed by. Nothing could create greater surprise and confusion among us than this! The wind was high and the sea was rough. We had our lower and middle deck guns closed in to protect them from the waves, so not a single gun on board was ready to fire at the French ships.

Two of the ships at the rear of our fleet saw what happened, and had time to prepare. They each gave the French ships a broadside as they passed by. It was not long before all our ships were prepared for an engagement.

Immediately, many things were tossed overboard to gain speed. The ships were made ready for fighting as soon as possible. At ten at night we hoisted a new main sail, as the old one had split. We were now ready for fighting, and so we chased the French fleet, which had one or two more ships than us.

We chased them all that night and at daylight, we saw six of them. They were all large ships of the line, and an English East Indiaman, which was a prize they had taken. We chased them all day until about three o'clock, when we passed within a musket shot of one seventy-four gun ship, which raised and then lowered her colours, which meant that she surrendered to us. We made a signal for the other ships to take possession of the East Indiaman. We all cheered, thinking that the man of war would also surrender, but she did not.

The French Commodore was only about a gun-shot ahead of our fleet, running from us with all speed when, about four o'clock, his foretopmast went overboard. This caused another loud cheer amongst our crew; and soon after her topmast also came away, as she was carrying all sail, to escape us. To our great surprise, instead of catching up with her, we found she went as fast as ever, if not faster. The sea grew much smoother and the wind calmer.

The French seventy-four gun ship we had passed came by us in the very same direction, so near, that we heard her people talk as she went by. Yet not a shot was fired on either side. About five or six o'clock, just as it grew dark, she joined her commodore. We chased all night; but the next day they were out of sight, and we saw no more of them. We only had the old Indiaman to show for our trouble.

After this, we stood in for the channel and soon made the land. At the close of the year 1758, we got safe to St. Helen's harbour. Here we ran aground but, by pouring our water overboard along with other things, we got the ships afloat again without any damage. We stayed for a short time at Spithead, and then went into Portsmouth harbour to refit. From Portsmouth, the admiral went to London. My master and I soon followed, with a press-gang, as we needed some more hands to complete our crew.

CHAPTER 4

BAPTISM AND BETRAYAL

It was now almost three years since I first came to England. I had spent most of that time at sea, and so became used to navy life. I even began to feel happy in my life, for my master always treated me extremely well. I felt a very great attachment and gratitude to him.

After all, I had seen aboard ships of war, I became a stranger to fear of any kind. In that respect at least, I became almost an Englishman. Despite the many dangers I had passed at sea, I never felt half the fear I was filled with when I first saw Europeans. At that time, every small act of theirs filled me with terror. That fear was due to my ignorance, which wore away as I began to know them.

I could now speak English quite well. I understood everything that was said perfectly. Not only did I feel easy with my new countrymen, but I also relished their society and manners. I no longer looked upon them as spirits, but as men more advanced than us. I, therefore, wanted to be like them - to drink in their spirit, and to imitate their manners.

I embraced every chance to learn, and every new thing that I saw was treasured in my memory. I longed to be able to read and write. I had taken every opportunity to learn but had made little progress as yet. However, when I went to London with my master, I soon had a chance to improve myself, which I gladly embraced. Shortly after my arrival, he sent me to wait on the young Guerin ladies, who had treated me with such kindness when I was there before. It was they who sent me to school.

While I was attending these ladies, their servants told me that I could not go to heaven unless I was baptised. This made me very uneasy, for I had now some faint idea of the afterlife. I told my worries to the eldest Miss Guerin and pressed her to have me baptized. To my great joy, she told me I should indeed be baptised.

She had in fact already asked my master to have me baptised, but he had refused. However, she now insisted upon it. Since my master owed a favour to her brother, he complied with her request. I was baptised in St. Margaret's church, Westminster, in February 1759, by my present name.

The clergyman, at the same time, gave me a book, called a Guide to the Indians, written by the Bishop of Sodor and Man. Miss Guerin did me the honour of becoming my godmother, and afterwards, she gave me a treat.

I used to act as servant to the Guerin ladies about London town, in which role I was extremely happy. This gave me many opportunities to see London, which I loved above all things. I was sometimes, however, with my master at his guesthouse, at the foot of Westminster bridge. Here, I used to enjoy myself in playing around the bridge steps, and in the watermen's boats, with some other boys.

One time, myself and another boy took a boat out into the current of the river. While we were there, two more stout boys came to us in another boat, and, abusing us for taking the boat, they told me to get into their boat. But just as I got one of my feet into the other boat, the boys shoved it off, so that I fell into the Thames. I couldn't swim and I would surely have drowned, but for the watermen who came to save me.

The Namur was soon again ready for sea and my master, and his gang of followers, were ordered on board. I was saddened to leave my schoolmaster, who I liked very much. I left the kind Guerin ladies with sadness. They often taught me reading, and taught me religion and the knowledge of God. I left those good ladies reluctantly. As we parted, they gave me friendly advice on how to conduct myself, and some fine presents.

When I came to Spithead, I was told that we were destined for the Mediterranean with a large fleet, which was ready to put to sea. We were only waiting for the admiral, who soon came on board. Early in the spring of 1759, we weighed anchor and got underway for the Mediterranean. Eleven days after Land's End we arrived in Gibraltar.

While we were there, I was often ashore, where there were various fruits in great plenty, and very cheap.

While ashore, I had often told people the story of my being kidnapped with my sister, and of our being separated. I often expressed my fears for her fate, and my sorrow at the thought of never meeting her again.

One day, when I was on shore, I told some people this story and one of them told me that he knew where my sister was. He said that if I would go with him, he would bring me to her. Unlikely as this story was, I believed it immediately. I agreed to go with him, while my heart leapt for joy. He brought me to a young black woman, who was so like my sister, that, at first sight, I really thought it was her. Yet I quickly learned the truth. On talking to her, I found that she was of another nation.

While we waited in Gibraltar, the Preston came in from Turkey. As soon as she arrived, my master said that I would now see my old friend, Dick, who had sailed with her for Turkey. I rejoiced at this news and expected to embrace him at any moment. I ran to inquire after my friend but, with inexpressible sorrow, I learned from the boat's crew that he was dead. They brought his chest, and all his other things, to my master. My master gave these things to me, and I saw them as a memorial of my friend, whom I loved, and grieved for, as a brother.

While we were at Gibraltar, I saw a soldier hanging by his heels, at one of the harbour walls. I thought strange, as I had seen a man hanged in London by his neck. Another time, I saw the master of a frigate towed to shore on a grating, by several of the men of war's boats, and discharged from the fleet. This was done as a mark of disgrace for cowardice. On board the same ship, there was also a sailor hung up at the yardarm.

After lying at Gibraltar for some time, we sailed up the Mediterranean a considerable way. Above the Gulf of Lyons we were one night overtaken by a terrible gale of wind, much greater than any I had ever before experienced. The sea ran so high that, though all the guns were well lashed down, there was reason to fear them getting loose, as the ship rolled so much. If the cannon had come loose, they could have destroyed the ship by smashing holes in her sides.

After we had cruised off the south of France for a time, we came to the Spanish sea-port of Barcelona. Here the ships were to take on water. As my master spoke several languages, he often interpreted for the admiral and oversaw the watering of our ship. The officers of the fleet had tents pitched in the bay and Spanish soldiers were stationed along the shore, to ensure that our men behaved themselves.

I was ashore constantly, attending upon my master. I was charmed with the place. All the time we were there, it was like being at a fair. The people brought us fruits of all kinds, which were much cheaper than in England. They also used to bring wine to us in sheepskins, which I enjoyed very much.

The Spanish officers treated our officers with great politeness. Some of them used to come to my master's tent to visit him, where they would sometimes amuse themselves by tying me onto the horses or mules, so I could not fall, before setting them off at full gallop. My lack of horsemanship gave them great entertainment.

After the ships were watered, we returned to our old station, cruising off Toulon to blockade the French fleet that lay there. One Sunday, we came to a place where two small French frigates lay close to shore. Our admiral wanted to take or destroy them. He sent two ships in after them, the Culloden and the Conqueror. They soon came upon to the Frenchmen and I saw a smart fight begin, by both sea and land. The French frigates were protected by cannon onshore, which fired furiously upon our ships, which returned fire just as furiously.

For a long time, a constant firing was kept up on all sides at an amazing rate. At last, one frigate sank, but the crew escaped, though not without difficulty. A little after, some of the crew left the other frigate too, which was by then a wreck. However, our ships did not try to take the ship away, as they were under fire from the shore batteries. Our ships' topmasts were shot away, and the ships were so shattered, that the admiral had to send many small boats to tow them back to the fleet.

After this, we sailed for Gibraltar, arriving there in August 1759. We stayed there while the fleet was watering and doing repairs. One day, about seven o'clock in the evening, we were heard signals being fired by the ships watching offshore. In an instant, there was a cry that the French fleet was out, and passing through the straits. The admiral rushed on board and it is impossible to describe the noise, hurry and confusion throughout the whole fleet, as we set sail and let go our ropes.

Many people and ships' boats were left on shore in the bustle. We had two captains on board of our ship who came away in the hurry, and left their ships to follow them. All our officers were busy telling the other ships not to wait for their captains, if they were ashore, but to put sails to the yards, slip their cables and follow us out. In such haste, we set out to sea in the dark, to chase the French fleet.

The French were so far ahead that we could not catch up with them during the night. At daybreak, we saw seven battle ships some miles ahead. We immediately chased them until about four o'clock that day, when our ships finally caught up with them. Although we had about fifteen large ships, our gallant admiral only fought them with his division of seven ships, to make sure that it was a fair fight, ship for ship.

We passed by the whole of the enemy fleet in order to come at their commander, Mons. La Clue, who was in the Ocean, an eighty-four gun ship. As we passed, they all fired on us and, at one time, three of them fired together. Despite this, our admiral would not allow a gun to be fired back at any of them, to my astonishment. Instead, he made us lie on our bellies on the deck until we were quite close to the Ocean, who was ahead of them all. Then, we were ordered to pour the whole of our three tiers of cannon into her at once.

The engagement now commenced with great fury on both sides. The Ocean immediately returned our fire, and we engaged with each other for some time. I was stunned by the thundering of the great guns, whose dreadful shot sent many of my friends into awful eternity.

At last, the French line was entirely broken, and we cheered our victory. We took three ships as prizes, La Modeste, of sixty-four guns, and Le Temeraire and Centaur, of seventy-four guns each. The rest of the French ships ran away, with all the sail they could carry. As our ship was very much damaged, the admiral left her, and went in the only boat we had left to board the Newark, to continue to chase the French with some other ships.

When trying to escape, the Ocean, and another large French ship, the Redoubtable, ran aground at Cape Logas on the coast of Portugal. The French admiral and some of his crew got ashore. We could not get the captured French ships afloat, so we set fire to them both. Around midnight, I saw the Ocean blow up, with a most dreadful explosion. I had never seen a more incredible sight. In a moment, midnight was turned into day by the blaze, which came with a noise louder and more terrible than thunder, which seemed to tear everything around us.

During the battle, I was on the middle-deck, where myself and another boy had the job of bringing powder to the rear gun. Here I saw the dreadful fate of many of my friends, who, in the twinkling of an eye, were cut to pieces, and launched into eternity.

Luckily, I escaped unhurt, though shot and splinters of wood flew thick about me during the whole fight. Towards the end of the battle, my master was wounded, and I saw him carried down to the surgeon. Although I was very worried about him and wished to help him, I dared not leave my post.

My gun mate and I ran the risk of blowing up the ship. When we took the cartridges out of the boxes, we found that the bottoms of many of them were rotten. The gunpowder ran all over the deck, just near the burning match tub, form which the cannon was lit.

Our work left us exposed to the enemy's fire, as we had run the whole length of the ship to get the gunpowder. I expected every moment to be my last when I saw so many of men fall about me.

At first I thought it would be safest not to go for gunpowder until the French had fired their broadside. Then, while they were reloading their cannon, I could run and get my powder. Then, I thought instead that this idea was pointless since I felt that there was a time set by fate for me to die, as well as to be born, I then cast off all fear and thoughts of death, and went swiftly to my duty. I was also made happy by the thought of telling tales of the battle to dear Miss Guerin, and others when I returned to London.

Our ship suffered very much in this fight. As well as the number of our people killed and wounded, the ship was almost torn to pieces, and our rigging was so shattered, that some of our masts and yards hung over the side of the ship. We had to get many carpenters from the other the ships in our fleet, to help set us in order.

Once we were refitted we sailed for England, with the prizes we had taken. During the passage, as soon as my master began to recover from his wounds, the admiral appointed him captain of the Aetna fire ship. We immediately left the Namur and went on board her at sea. I liked this little ship very much. I now became the captain's steward, in which role I was very happy. I was extremely well treated by all on board and I had plenty of time to improve my reading and writing.

I had learned some writing before I left the Namur, as there was a school on board. When we arrived at Spithead, the Aetna went into Portsmouth harbour to refit. Once that was done, we returned to Spithead and joined a large fleet that was to sail against the Havannah, but about that time the king died. Whether the king's death stopped the expedition I do not know, but we had to wait for orders.

Our ship was stationed in Cowes, on the Isle of Wight, until the beginning of the 1761. Here I spent my time very pleasantly. I spent much time ashore exploring this delightful island, where I found the people very kind. While I was there, a happy thing happened. One day, I was playing in a field. By coincidence, this field belonged to a gentleman who had a black boy about my own age. This boy had seen me from his master's house and was delighted to see one of his own countrymen. He ran to meet me in a great hurry. When I saw someone running at me, I wasn't sure what was happening, so I went to run away at first, but he soon came close to me and caught hold of me in his arms, as if I was his brother, even though we had never seen one another before.

After we had talked together for some time, he took me to his master's house, where I was treated very kindly. This kind boy and I were very happy to often meet and play together, until March 1761, when our ship received orders to fit out for another expedition.

Once the ship was ready, we joined a very large fleet at Spithead. This fleet was commanded by Commodore Keppel. We were to attack the French island of Belle Isle, and land troops on the island. We sailed out once more, in quest of fame. I longed for new adventures and see fresh wonders.

I had a curious mind. Every event, and everything unusual, made a strong impression on me. I saw the hand of God in each extraordinary escape, of either myself or others. We were less than ten days at sea before such an incident happened, which made a real impression on my mind.

We had on board a gunner, whose name was John Mondle. He was a man of questionable morals. His cabin was between the decks, exactly above where I lay. On the night of 20th of April, he awoke from a nightmare in so great a fright that he could not lie in bed any longer, nor even stay in his cabin. He went on deck about four o'clock in the morning, extremely agitated.

He told those on deck of the agony in his mind, and the dream which caused it. In his dream, he had seen many awful things, and had been warned by St. Peter to repent, for time was short. This had greatly alarmed him, and he was determined to change his life.

People generally mock the fears of others, when they are themselves in safety. Some of our shipmates who heard his story laughed at him. However, he made a vow that he never would drink strong liquors again. He immediately took a lamp, and gave away his stores of liquor.

After this, he began to read the bible, hoping to find some relief. He laid himself down again on his bed, and tried to sleep, but couldn't, for his mind was still in agony.

By this time it was exactly half-past seven in the morning. I was by the great cabin door when I suddenly heard people fearfully cry out, "Lord have mercy upon us! We are all lost! The Lord have mercy upon us!"

Mr. Mondle heard the cries and immediately ran out of his cabin, when we were instantly struck by the Lynne, a forty-gun ship. Before Mr. Mondle had taken four steps from his cabin-door, the Lynne struck our ship, and her cutwater right in the middle of his bed and cabin. In a minute, there was not a bit of wood to be seen where Mr. Mondle's cabin had been. He was so close to being killed that some of the splinters tore his face.

Mr. Mondle would certainly have died, had he not been warned in this very strange way. I felt awe at this, which I saw as the work of God. This close escape of Mr. Mondle had a great influence on his life ever after.

The two ships swung alongside, tangled badly each other. Our ship was in such a shocking condition that we all thought she would instantly go down. Everyone ran for their lives and went on board the Lynne.

When she did not sink immediately, the captain went on board again, and encouraged us to return and try to save her. Many went back, but some would not.

Some ships in the fleet sent their boats to help us, but it took us the whole day to save the ship. We tied her together with many ropes, and put a great amount of tar below the waterline, where she was damaged. She barely kept together, and any gale of wind would have sent her to pieces. We were in such a crazy condition that we needed ships to attend us until we arrived at Belle Isle, where she was properly repaired.

As I am on the subject, I'll tell a couple of other stories which cause me firmly believe in heavenly intervention. In 1758, I was sailing on Jason, of fifty-four guns, near Plymouth. One night, a woman, with a child at her breast, fell from the upper-deck down into the hold, near the keel. Everyone thought that the mother and child must be dead but, to our great surprise, neither was hurt.

I myself one day fell headlong from the upper-deck of the Aetna down into the hold, when the ballast was out. All who saw me fall cried out that I was killed, but I hadn't the slightest least injury. In the same ship, a man fell from the mast-head to the deck without being hurt. In these, and many other cases, I could plainly see the hand of God, without whose permission a sparrow cannot fall.

I began to raise my fears from man to him alone, and to call daily on his holy name with fear and reverence. I trust he heard my prayers, and answered me by planting the seeds of piety in me, one of the humblest of his creatures.

When we had repaired our ship, and were ready to assault the island, the troops on board the transports were ordered to attack. My master, as a junior captain, was involved in commanding the landing. This was on the 8th of April. The French were on the shore, ready to defend against our attack. Our men fought with great bravery, but they became cut off, and many were taken prisoners. Our lieutenant was also killed.

On 21 April, we again tried to land the men, while the men of war were stationed along the shore to protect them. We fired at the French batteries from early morning until about four o'clock, when our soldiers effected a safe landing. They immediately attacked the French and soon forced them from the batteries.

Before the French retreated, they blew up several of their own guns, so we could not use them. Our men laid siege around the fortress, and my master was ordered ashore to organise the landing of everything needed for the siege. I went ashore to help him.

We now held all the island, except the fortress. When I had time, I went to explore different parts of the island. One day, my curiosity almost cost me my life. I wondered how mortars were loaded, so I went to an English battery that was near the walls of the French fortress.

There, I saw the whole operation of loading the mortars, but we came under attack from the French. One of their largest shells exploded just ten yards from me. There was a single rock close by, about the size of a barrel, and I took shelter under it, just in time to avoid the fury of the shell. Where it exploded, the earth was torn open wide, throwing heaps of stones and dirt a great distance. Three musket shots were also fired at me, and another boy who was with me.

One of them in particular seemed to fly with lightning rage. With a most dreadful sound it hissed close by me, and struck a nearby rock, shattered it to pieces. When I saw the danger I was in, I tried to escape the quickest way I could. An English sergeant, who commanded the outposts, reprimanded me very severely for sneaking in front of the lines, and arrested the sentry for letting me pass.

I then noticed a horse, belonging to one of the islanders. I had an idea to mount it, to get away quickly. I took some rope which I had with me, and made a kind of bridle with it. I put it around the horse's head, and the tame creature very quietly let me harness and mount him. As soon as I was on the horse's back, I began to kick and beat him, to make him go quick. All this was of little use as he would only walk at a slow pace. While I was creeping along, still within reach of the enemy's shot, I met a servant on a fine English horse.

I immediately stopped and, crying, told him my story. I begged him to help me, and this he did. With his fine large whip, he began to lash my horse so severely, that he set off full speed with me towards the sea. I was unable to control him and I flew along, towards a craggy cliff edge. I couldn't stop the horse and my mind filled with the thought of my terrible fate, if the horse were go down the cliff, which he seemed about to do. I thought I had better throw myself off him at once, which I did with some skill, and so I escaped unhurt. I made the way to the ship, promising myself that I would not be so foolish again.

We continued to besiege the fortress until June, when it finally surrendered. During the siege, I had counted above sixty shells in the air at once. When the fortress was taken I went through the citadel, and the bomb-proof shelters under it, which were cut into the solid rock. I thought it an amazing place, both for its strength and how it was built – even though our shots and shells had caused devastation, and heaps of rubble all around it.

After we took the island of Belle Isle, our ships joined a fleet for Basse-road, where we blocked in a French fleet. Our ships were there from June until the following February. In that time, I saw a many scenes of war, and many clever strategies by both sides to destroy each other's ships. Sometimes we would attack the French with our largest ships, at other times with boats. We often took French ships as prizes.

Once or twice, the French attacked us by firing shells with their bomb boats. One day as a French vessel was firing shells at our ships, she broke from her ropes, behind the Isle de Re. The tide took her within a gun shot of our ship, the Nassau, but the Nassau could not aim cannon at her in time, and so the Frenchman got away. We were twice attacked by their fire-floats, which they chained together, and lit, before letting them float down with the tide. Each time, we sent boats with grappling hooks to attach to the burning rafts, and towed them safely away out of the way of the fleet.

In February 1762 we went back to Belle-Isle, and there stayed until summer, when we returned to Portsmouth. After our ship was fitted out again for service, in September we sailed to Guernsey. I was delighted to see my old hostess, who was now a widow, and my charming little friend, her daughter.

I spent some happy times with them, until October, when we had orders to sail to Portsmouth. We parted with a great deal of affection, and I promised to return soon, and see them again - not knowing then what fate had decided for me.

Our ship having arrived at Portsmouth, and we went into the harbour, where we stayed until the end of November, when we heard great talk about peace. To our great joy, at the beginning of December, we received orders to go up to London with our ship to be paid off, as the war was over at last.

We received this news with loud cheers, and nothing but jot was to be seen through every part of the ship. I thought now of nothing but being freed, and working for myself, to get money for a good education. I always had a great desire to be able to read and write, at least.

While I was at sea, I had worked to improve my reading and writing. While I was in the Aetna, the captain's clerk taught me to write, and taught me a smattering of maths too. There was also a man named Daniel Queen, about forty years of age, who was very well educated. He ate with me on board this ship, and he served and attended the captain. He soon became fond of me, and taught me many things. He taught me to shave and dress my hair a little, and also to read the Bible, explaining many passages to me.

I was wonderfully surprised to see the laws and rules of my country written almost exactly in the Bible. This helped me to remember my people's manners and customs. I used to tell him of this similarities, and we often sat up the whole night together speaking of such things. Before long, some people began to call me the black Christian.

Daniel Queen was like a father to me. I loved him almost as a son would. I gave him many gifts. If I won a few half pennies at marbles or any other game, or got any little money for shaving someone, I used to buy him a little sugar or tobacco. He used to say, that he and I never should part. He said that once our ship was paid off, I would be as free as any other man on board. He said that he would teach me his business, so that I would have a good livelihood.

This gave me new life and spirits. My heart burned within me, even though freedom still seemed far in the future. My master had not promised freedom to me yet, even though I was told that the laws of England gave him no right to enslave me there.

Yet my master always treated me with the greatest kindness. He even paid attention to my morals and would never allow me to deceive him, or to tell lies. He told me that that if I did so, God would not love me. Because of all this kindness, I had never once imagined, in all my dreams of freedom, that he would even think of keeping me a slave any longer than I wished.

We were ordered to sail from Portsmouth to the Thames. We arrived at Deptford on 10 December, where we cast anchor at high water. My master ordered the barge to be manned. Then, in an instant, without having before given me any reason to fear such a thing, he forced me into the barge. He said he knew I planned to leave him, but that he would make sure I did not.

I was so struck with shock, that couldn't speak. I asked if I could get my books and my chest of clothes, but he said he would cut my throat if I left his sight.

I began to tried to calm myself. Plucking up courage, I told him I was free, and that he could not by law treat me this way. But this only enraged him more and he continued to swear. He said he would soon show me, and he jumped into the barge from the ship, and took me into the barge, to the sadness of all on board.

The tide, rather unluckily for me, had just turned downward, so that we quickly fell down the river along with it, until we came among some ships bound for the

West Indies. He said he would to put me on board the first ship he could get to take me.

The barge's crew, pulled the oars unwillingly, and would have gone ashore but he would not let them. Some of them tried to cheer me up, and told me he could not sell me, and that they would stand by me. This revived my spirits a little, and I still had hope. As they rowed along, he asked some ships to receive me, but they could not. But, just as we went a past Gravesend, we came alongside a ship which was going to the West Indies on the next tide. Her name was the Charming Sally. My master went aboard and agreed a price for me with the Captain of the ship, James Doran.

I was soon sent into the captain's cabin. When I arrived, Captain Doran asked me if I knew him. I answered that I did not. "Then," said he "you are now my slave." I told him my master could not sell me to him, nor to anyone else.

"Why," said he, "did your master not buy you?" I admitted that he did. I said, "But I have served him many years, and he has taken all my wages and prize-money, for I only got one sixpence during the war. Besides, I have been baptised and, by the laws of the land, no man has a right to sell me." I added, that I had heard a lawyer and others tell my master so.

They both then said that those who told me this were not my friends. I replied that it was extraordinary that they knew the law better than others. At this, Captain Doran said I talked too much English and that, if I did not behave myself well, and be quiet, he had a ways to make me do so.

I was convinced of his power over me, and did not doubt what he said, My sufferings in the slave-ship now came to mind, and the memory of them made me shudder. I told them that, as I could not get any justice amongst men, I hoped I would in Heaven.

I left the cabin, filled with resentment and sorrow. The only coat I had with me, my master took away with him, saying that if my prize-money had been £10,000, he had a right to it all, and that he would have taken it. I had about nine guineas, which, during my long sea-faring life, I had scraped together from my little ventures. I hid it that instant, in case my master should take that from me too, still hoping that I might make my escape to the shore.

Some of my old shipmates told me not to despair, and that would get me free again and that, as soon as they could get their pay, they would come to Portsmouth to get me, as this ship would stop there on the way to the West Indies. Yet the hour of my deliverance was far off.

My master, having struck his bargain with the captain, came out of the cabin, got into the barge and set off. I followed them with aching eyes for as long as I could. When they went out of sight, I threw myself down on the deck, with a heart was ready to burst with sorrow and anguish.

CHAPTER 5

1763 TO 1766: A NEW SLAVERY

Just when expected that my toil to end, I was plunged into a new slavery. The horrors of my first enslavement had always been at the back of my mind, but these thoughts now rushed viciously upon me. This new slavery made the old one seem like perfect freedom. I wept bitterly for a long time.

I wondered if I had done something to displease God, to deserve such severe punishment. I thought about all that I had done. I remembered that when I arrived in Deptford, I had sworn that I'd spend the day in rambling and sport, as soon I reached London. My conscience now struck me for these unwise words.

I felt God's power over my life, and I saw my second enslavement as a judgment of Heaven for my swearing. I admitted my wrongdoing to God and poured out my soul before him in deep repentance. I begged him no him not to abandon me in my distress.

Before long, my grief seemed to burn itself out with its own fury. I began to think more calmly about my situation. I thought that adversity can sometimes be sent for our good. I thought God might have allowed this to happen to teach me wisdom and acceptance. After all, God had sheltered me with the wings of his mercy, and his invisible hand guided me in ways I could not understand. These thoughts gave me some comfort. I rose from the deck with dejection and sorrow on my face, yet with some faint hope that God would free me in the end.

Soon afterwards, my new master was going ashore. He called me to him, and told me to behave myself, and that it would be best for me if I worked just like the rest of the boys. I didn't answer. He asked if I could swim, and I said I couldn't.

I was made to go below decks, where I was carefully watched. On the next tide, the ship got underway, and we soon arrived at Portsmouth, where we waited for the West India convoy for a few days.

While in Portsmouth, I tried everything to persuade the crew to get me a boat from the shore, as none were allowed to come alongside of the ship. The ship's own boat was hoisted aboard again as soon as it was used. A sailor on board took a guinea from me on the pretence of getting me a boat. He promised me, time and again, that it was soon to arrive.

When he was on watch on deck, I watched too. I looked long enough but never saw either the boat or my guinea again. Worst of all, this fellow told the crew of my plan to escape. Yet he never told them he had taken a guinea from me to help me escape. Later on, after we had sailed, this trick became known to the ship's crew. I was pleased to see how he became hated by all for how he had tricked me.

While in Portsmouth, I still hoped that my old shipmates would remember their promise to come for me there. Indeed, on the day before we sailed, some of them did come. They sent me some oranges and other things. They also sent me word they would come to get me the next day, or the day after. A lady who lived in Gosport wrote to tell me that she would help my shipmates come and take me from of the ship. This lady had been once very close to my former master. I used to take care of a great deal of business for her, in different ships. She always showed great friendship to me, and used to tell my master that she would take me away to live with her one day. Unfortunately for me, they argued soon afterwards. My old master then became close to another lady, who often stayed on board the Aetna. This lady took against me, and turned my old master against me too, encouraging him to treat me as he did.

The next morning, the 30th of December, the wind was brisk and easterly. The Oeolus frigate, which was to escort the convoy, made a signal for sailing. All the ships then took up their anchors and, before any of my friends could come to rescue me, our ship got under way

An unspeakable anguish troubled my soul as the convoy got under sail. I was now without hope, a prisoner on board. I kept my eyes upon the land in a state of grief, not knowing what to do, or how to help myself. While my mind was in this state, the fleet sailed on. In one day's time, I lost sight of that much wished-for land.

In my grief, I wished I had never been born. I was ready to curse the tide that carried us, the breeze that wafted my prison along, and even the ship that carried us. I called upon death to relieve me from the horrors I felt and dreaded. I begged to die, to be in that place where slaves are free, and men oppress no more. In time, my emotions however gave way to calmer thoughts. I soon understood that no one can prevent the workings of fate.

The convoy sailed on, with a pleasant wind and smooth sea, for six weeks until February. One night, the Oeolus crashed into ship in the convoy, which instantly went down, engulfed by the dark ocean. The convoy was immediately thrown into great confusion, until day broke. The Oeolus was lit with lights to prevent any other accidents.

On 13 February 1763, the crew at the mast-head, cried out that they saw our destination, the island of Montserrat. I soon saw that dark place of sorrow, "where peace and rest can rarely dwell. Hope never comes … but torture without end".

At the sight of this land of slavery, a fresh horror ran through my body and chilled my heart. Memories of my former slavery now arose in fearfully in my mind. I saw nothing but misery, whips, and chains. In this rush of grief, I called upon God's thunder to bring death to me, rather than allow me to become a slave, to be sold from master to master.

In this state of mind, our ship came to anchor, and we soon began the hard work of unloading her cargo. I was made to help to unload the ship. And, to comfort me in my distress, two of the sailors robbed me of all my money, and ran away from the ship.

I had become so used to the European climate that the scorching sun of the West Indies felt very painful at first. As we unloaded the ship onto the beach, the breaking surf would often toss our boat and its crew onto the shore. Sometimes, people's limbs were broken, or they were killed instantly. Every day, I was mangled and torn by this work.

About the middle of May, the ship was ready to sail for England. All this time, I felt   fate's blackest clouds gathering above my head. I expected them to soon burst, and mix me with the dead.

One morning, Captain Doran sent for me to come ashore. The messenger told me that my fate had been decided. With weak steps, and a trembling heart, I went to the captain. I found with him a Mr. Robert King, who was a Quaker, and the leading merchant of Montserrat.

The captain told me my former master had sent me to Montserrat to be sold, asking that I be given the best master possible, as I was a very deserving boy. Captain Doran said he had found this to be true. He said that, if he were staying in the West Indies, he would gladly keep me himself. Yet he could not risk taking me to London, for he was sure that I would leave him there. At this, I burst out crying, and begged him to take me to England, but it was no use.

Captain Doran told me he had got me the very best master on the whole island. He said I would be as happy with him as I would have been in England. He said this is why he was giving me to Mr King, even though he could sell me to his own brother-in-law for far more money.

Mr. King, my new master, then said that he had bought me because of my good character. He said that because he knew I'd behave well, I would do well with him. He also told me that he did not live in the West Indies, but at Philadelphia, where he was going soon. He said that since

I understood some mathematics, he would put me to school there, and train me to become a clerk.

This conversation relieved my mind a little. I left those gentlemen more at ease in myself than when I came to them. I was very grateful to Captain Doran, and even to my old master, for what they had said about me. Their good reference was later to be of great service to me.

I went on board again and said goodbye to all my shipmates. The next day, the ship sailed. As she sailed away, I went to the waterside and looked at her with an aching heart. I followed her with tears in my eyes, until she was out of sight. I was so bowed down with grief that I could not hold up my head for many months. If my new master had not been kind to me, I think my grief would have killed me at last.

I soon found that my new master fully deserved the good words which Captain Doran had said about him. He was friendly and calm, and was very generous and humane. If any of his slaves misbehaved, he did not beat them, but sold them. This made them afraid of upsetting him. Because he treated his slaves better than any other man on the island, he was better served by them in return. In time, I began to feel able to face whatever fate had in store for me with strength.

Mr. King said he did not intend to treat me as a common slave and asked me what I could do. I told him I knew seamanship, and could shave and cut hair pretty well. I said I could refine wines, and that I could write, and understood maths reasonably well. He asked if I knew anything of accounting. When I said I did not, he said one of his clerks would teach me this.

Mr. King dealt in all sorts of merchandise. He had up to six clerks. He loaded many ships every year. These often sailed to Philadelphia, where he was born. He had connections with a great merchant house in that city.

Mr King also had many vessels and barges of different sizes, which used to go about the island to collect rum, sugar and other goods. I knew how to sail these boats, and so this was the work he first set me to. In the sugar season, I rowed these boat up to sixteen hours a day. I was usually given fifteen pence per day to live on, but sometimes only ten pence. Yet even this was far more than most other slaves who worked with me got. The poor souls who belonged to other gentlemen on the island never got more than nine pence per day, and usually got less than six pence - even though they earned 36 or 48 pence a day for their masters. It is common in the West Indies for men to purchase slaves, even though they have not plantations themselves, to rent them out to planters and merchants by the day.

They often give a scanty allowance to their slaves to feed themselves. My master often gave the owners of these slaves 30 pence per day for the slaves, but he fed the poor fellows too, because he thought their owners did not feed them well enough. The slaves used to like this. They knew that my master was a man of feeling, and so they were always preferred work for him over any other gentleman.

Some of the slave owners would not give their slaves any allowance out of the pay they received for their work. I saw these unfortunate wretches being beaten many time, for asking for their pay. They were often severely flogged by their owners if they did not bring them their daily or weekly money exactly on time. This happened, even though the poor creatures had to sometimes wait more than half a day to get paid. This often happened on Sundays, when the gentlemen wanted time to themselves.

I knew a countryman of mine who did not bring the weekly money immediately, even though he brought it to his master that day. For this supposed wrong, he was staked to the ground and was just about to receive a hundred lashes when a gentleman intervened and asked that the poor man only be given fifty lashes.

This poor slave was very industrious. He even managed to earn so much money by working on shipboard, that he got a white man to buy him a boat - unknown to his master. Sometime after, the governor wanted a boat to bring his sugar from different parts of the island. Knowing it to be a black man's boat, the governor seized it for himself, and would not pay the owner a penny.

The man went to his master and complained about what the governor had done. He was to be damned heartily by his master, who asked him how any of his black people dared to have a boat. It may be a consolation to this poor man, to know that the governor soon lost his fortune. I was told the governor later died in England, in great poverty. It seems that theft is a poor provider.

The recent war had gone well for this poor black man, and he escaped from his Christian master. He later came to England, where I saw him several times. Cruelty often drives these poor people to despair, and they risk their lives to run away from their masters. When unable to get their pay after they earned it, and fearing to be flogged if they returned home without it, many would run away. A reward was then often offered to bring them back, dead or alive. My master often arranged to pay their owners directly, which saved many from a flogging.

Once, I was rented out for a few days to fit out a vessel. Yet I was given no food while at this work. In the end, I told my master how I was being treated, and he took me away from this job. On the islands where I used to go for rum or sugar, many of the plantations would not deliver goods to me, or any other black man. My master had to send a white man along with me to those places, who was paid up to 12 shillings a day.

As I spent my days going about the different estates on the island, I saw the dreadful way the poor slaves were treated. Seeing this, made me thank God that I had fallen into my master's hands.

I pleased my master in all the work he gave me. There was hardly any part of his affairs which I was not involved in. I often worked as a clerk, receiving and delivering cargoes to ships, tending stores and delivering goods. I also used to shave and dress my master, and take care of his horse. I often worked on board his many ships. I became very useful to my master. He used to say that I saved him over a hundred pounds a year. He also said that I was better than any of his other clerks, even though they earned up to a hundred pounds a year.

I have heard it said that a slave cannot earn his master what he costs. Nothing could be further from the truth. I imagine that 90 percent of the skilled tradesmen in the West Indies are black slaves. Many of these are barrel-makers and carpenters, who earn two dollars a day for their masters. Many are stonemasons, blacksmiths and fishermen. I have known many slaves whose masters would not sell them for a thousand pounds.

Surely the idea that a slave cannot repay what he costs refutes itself. If it were true, why would planters and merchants pay what they do for slaves? Above all, why do those who make such claims argue loudly against abolishing the slave trade?

I admit that when slaves are only half-fed, barely clothed, overworked and whipped, they can become reduced so low, that become unfit for service. They are then left to die in the woods, or on a dunghill.

My master was offered one hundred guineas for me several times. He always said he would never sell me, to my great joy. I used to then work doubly hard, for fear of getting into the hands of men who would not give a slave what he needs to live. Many used to criticise my master for feeding his slaves as well as he did. Although, I often went hungry, and an Englishman would think my food very poor. Yet he used to say he would always feed his slaves well, because it meant they looked better, and did more work.

In the Caribbean, I saw all kinds of cruelties done to my fellow slaves. I often had cargoes of new black people in my care, who were to be sold. Our clerks, and other whites, almost constantly violently sexually assaulted the female slaves. I was unable to help them.

When we had female slaves on board my master's vessels, to carry them to other islands, or to America, our crew would commit these acts most shamefully. This was to the disgrace, not only of Christians, but of all men. I have even known them to indulge their brutal passions with females not ten years old. Some did these abominations to such excess, that one of our captains discharged the mate and others because of it.

Yet in Montserrat I saw a black man staked to the ground, and cut horrifically. His ears were then cut off bit by bit, because he had been with a white woman, who was a common prostitute. It was no crime for the whites to rob an innocent African girl of her virtue. Yet it was

95

considered evil for a black man to gratify a passion of nature, with one of a different colour, even if she was the least innocent woman.

Another black man was half hanged, and then burnt, for attempting to poison a cruel overseer. Through repeated cruelties, the slaves are first made to despair. They are then murdered - simply because they retain enough human nature to want to put an end to their misery, and retaliate against their tyrants.

Most of these overseers are people of the worst character of any sort of men in the West Indies. Unfortunately, many humane gentlemen do not live on their estates, and so leave the management of them in the hands of these human butchers. Such men treat the slaves like animals, and cut and mangle them in a shocking manner for the smallest thing. They don't care about pregnant women, or where the field slaves live. Their huts, which ought to be well covered and dry, are often just open sheds, built in damp places. This means that when the poor creatures return tired from the toils of the field, they contract diseases, from being exposed to elements.

This neglect means shorter lives for the adults and fewer births. I know of many cases where, when the gentlemen who own the estates come to stay, everything changes. Then, the slaves are treated leniently and with proper care. This means that their lives are prolonged, which increases their masters profit.

To the honour of humanity, I knew several gentlemen who managed their estates in a humane way, and proved that kindness was in their true interest. I knew one in Montserrat whose slaves looked remarkably well. The estate never needed any fresh supplies of black people. There are many other estates, especially in Barbados, which, never need fresh stocks of slaves, as they treat their people well.

I know a worthy and humane gentleman, who is a native of Barbados, and has estates there. He has written about how he treats his own slaves. He allows them two hours rest at midday, and many comforts. He grows more food on his estate than they can use, so that he saves the lives of his slaves, and keeps them as healthy and happy as it's possible for people who are enslaved to be.

I myself later managed an estate where good treatment meant that the black people were unusually cheerful and healthy. They did more work by half than those who are treated in the usual way. The lack of care and attention to the poor black people is so great that it is no wonder that the island needs 20,000 new slaves annually to take the places of the dead.

Barbados is known to be the place where slaves get the best treatment. It therefore needs the fewest new recruits of any island in the West Indies. Yet even this island needs 1,000 slaves annually to keep up its original stock, which is only 80,000.

Despite the humane masters I have mentioned, many black people only live to sixteen years of age there. And yet the climate in the Caribbean is the same as that in Africa, from here they were taken. Do the British colonies decrease in this manner? And yet what a huge difference is there between the climate in England and the West Indies.

While I was in Montserrat, I knew a black man named Emanuel Sankey, who tried to escape from his miserable bondage, by concealing himself on board a ship for London. Fate did not favour the poor man. He was discovered when the vessel was under sail, and was sent back to his master. This Christian master immediately pinned the wretch down to the ground at each wrist and ankle. He then took some sticks of wax, and lit them, dropping the hot wax all over his back.

There was another master who was noted for cruelty. I believe all of his slaves had been cut, and had pieces taken out of their flesh. After they had been punished in this way, he used to make them get into a long wooden box, the size of a coffin. He then locked them up in this for as long as he pleased. The poor wretches had no room to move.

It was common in St Kitts, and many islands, for the slaves to be branded with their master's initials. Many had a load of heavy iron hooks hung about their necks. Over the smallest thing, they were loaded with chains, and instruments of torture were often added. The iron muzzle and thumb-screws are so well known as not to need a description. These were sometimes applied for the slightest faults. I have seen a black man beaten until his bones were broken, for letting a pot boil over. Is it surprising that treatment like this should drive the poor creatures to despair, and make them seek escape in death from those evils which make their lives unbearable?

Shuddering with pale horror, their eyes aghast, they view their lamentable lot, and find no rest.

The poem, The Dying Negro tells the tale of a black man, who ran away from his master, and became baptised, so that he marry a white woman he loved, who was a fellow-servant. He was caught, taken on board a ship in the Thames, and in despair shot himself through the head. I myself have seen how slaves are often driven to seek death.

When I was on board one of my master's vessels, a black man who had been put in irons for some small thing, was kept chained up for days. Becoming weary of life, he managed to jump overboard into the sea. However, he was picked up before he drowned. Another, whose life also became a burden to him, resolved to starve himself to death, and refused to eat any food. He was severely flogged for this. He also jumped overboard as soon has he could, but was saved.

These are just a few of the many instances of oppression I have seen. The following cruelty is common on all the islands. The poor field-slaves, after working all day for an uncaring owner, who gives them little food, sometimes take a few moments to gather a small portion of grass. They usually tie this up as a parcel and bring it to the market to sell.

The white people usually simply take the grass from them without paying for it. At the same time, the men often violate the poor, wretched, and helpless females. I have seen them stand and cry for hours without end. They get no justice or pay of any kind.

Is this not enough to bring down God's judgment on the islands? God tells us the oppressor and the oppressed are both in his hands. If these are not the poor, the broken-hearted, the blind, the captive, the bruised, which our Saviour speaks of, who are they?

In St. Eustatia, one of these evil men came on board of our vessel, and bought some fowls and pigs from me. They next day he came back and wanted his money back. I refused to give it. My captain was not on board, and he began to play usual tricks on me. He said he would break open my chest and take my money.

I expected that he would be as good as his word. He was just about to strike me, when fortunately a British seaman came on board, whose heart had not been hardened by the West India climate. He stopped the attack. Had the cruel man struck me I certainly should have defended myself, even at the risk of being hanged for doing so. For what value has life to a man who is so oppressed? This man went away swearing that when he caught me on shore he would shoot me, and pay for me afterwards.

It's well known what little value is placed upon the life of a black person in the West Indies. Yet some are brazen enough to claim that that black people are nowadays treated equally to Europeans. Let me show you the proof that this idea is false. The law of the Assembly of Barbados says that a master who kills a slave while punishing him need not pay a fine. Yet if any other man "out of wantonness, or only of bloody-mindedness, or cruel intention" kills a black person, he must pay a fine of fifteen pounds. It is the same in most, if not all, of the West Indies.

Does the assembly which made this law not deserve to be called savages and brutes, rather than Christians and men? Such a law is at once unmerciful, unjust, and unwise. It would disgrace an assembly of barbarians for its cruelty. Its injustice and insanity would shock the morality and common sense of a wild man.

Shocking as this, and many more laws of the bloody West Indies appear at first glance, it's worth considering how their evil is heightened, when such laws are applied even to the children of the slavers. Mr. James Tobin, tells how a French planter on the island of St Martin, showed him many mixed-race slaves working in the fields, like beasts of burden. He told Mr. Tobin that these were all his own children. I myself have known similar cases. Are these sons and daughters of the French planter less his children by being born to a black woman? What must the morals of those lawmakers, and the feelings of those fathers, who thinks the lives of their children as being worth no more than fifteen pounds if they be murdered, as the law says, "*out of wantonness and bloody-mindedness*". Is the slave trade not at war with the very heart of man? Surely a trade that begins by breaking down goodness must continue to destroy every principle and to bury all kindness in utter ruin.

I have often seen slaves put onto scales and weighed, especially if they are thin. They are then sold for as little as three pence a pound. My master's humanity was shocked at this way of selling slaves, and so he used to sell them by the batch. After a sale, it was not uncommon to see men taken from their wives, wives taken from their husbands, and children from their parents.

They were then sent off to other islands, or wherever else their merciless lords chose. Most never saw each other again in this life. My heart bled at these partings, when the friends of the departed went to the waterside, and - with sighs and tears - kept their eyes fixed on the ship until it went out of sight.

A poor mixed-race man I knew well had often been transported from island to island in this way, until he was brought to Montserrat. This man told me many sad tales of his life. In the evenings, after he had finished working for his master, he often spent his few of moments leisure in fishing.

When he caught some fish, his master would often take them from him without paying him. Sometimes, other white people did the same thing. One day he said to me, very movingly, "Sometimes when a white man take away my fish I go to my maser, and he get me my right, and when my maser by strength take away my fishes, what me must do? I can't go to anybody to be righted, then". The poor man said, looking up above, "I must look up to God Mighty in the top for right."

This simple tale moved me, and I could not help feeling the justice of Moses' cause against the Egyptians who held his people in slavery. I told the man to keeping looking up to the God on the top, as there was no justice here below. Although I never thought then that I should soon experience such injustices, I did. Indeed, this poor man and I were soon to suffer together.

I visited fifteen West Indies islands, and the treatment of the slaves was nearly the same everywhere. The slave-trade to corrupts men's minds, and hardens them to every feeling of humanity. I don't think the dealers in slaves were born worse than other men. No, it is greed which corrupts the milk of human kindness and turns it into poison. Had the lives of those men been different, they might have been generous, kind-hearted and fair, instead of unfeeling, greedy and cruel.

The slave trade spreads like a disease and corrupts all it touches. It violates the natural rights of mankind: equality and freedom. It gives one man a control over others, which God could never intend.

It raises the owner above the level of an ordinary human, just as it pushes the slave below that level. Human pride then creates a vast distinction between them. How mistaken is the greed of the planters? Are slaves made more useful by being treated as animals, rather than as humans?

The freedom which spreads health and prosperity across Britain – where slavery is banned - proves that it does not. When you make men slaves, you deprive them of half their virtue. You teach them by your own deception, greed, and cruelty. You make them live in a state of war with you - yet you complain that they are not honest or faithful. You stupefy them with the lashes of the whip, and keep them in a state of ignorance. Yet you say that they are unable to learn, and that that their minds are barren and that culture would be lost on them. You say that they come from a climate where nature has left humans unfinished, and unable to enjoy the treasures of the world. This is absurd and wrong.

Why do you use instruments of torture? It is right for one rational being to use them against another? Are you not struck with shame, to see humans become so low? Above all, is it not dangerous to treat people this way? Are you not afraid of a slave rebellion? Nor would that be surprising, when no peace is given to them. But by changing your conduct, and treating your slaves as humans, this fear would be relieved. They would be faithful, honest, intelligent and hardworking. In peace, prosperity and happiness, they would look after you.

Chapter 6

DREAMS OF FREEDOM

I have only told a few stories of the cruelty I saw in the West Indies. If I were to tell you everything, it would disgust you too much. The routine punishment of slaves for the smallest thing is well known, as are the instruments with which they are tortured. It is not news to tell of such things. Yet they are so shocking for both the writer and the reader that, from now on, I will only mention the cruelties which I personally experienced during my adventures.

In the many jobs I did for my master, I saw many strange things on the islands. Yet of all these, I was especially struck by Brimstone Hill, which is a high and steep mountain, a few miles from the town of Plymouth in Montserrat. I had often heard tales of the wonders that were to be seen on this hill, so I once went there with a group of white and black people.

When we arrived on the hilltop, we saw cliffs and great molten rocks of brimstone. Steam rose from many little ponds, which were boiling in the earth. Some of these ponds were as white as milk, others were blue and multicoloured. I had brought some potatoes with me, which I put into different ponds. In just a few minutes, they were well boiled. I tasted them, but they tasted of sulphur. Our silver shoe buckles and every other metal thing we had with us were soon turned as black as lead.

In 1763, fate seemed to favour me. One of my master's vessels, a Bermudan sloop of sixty tons, was commanded by one Captain Thomas Farmer. He was a very active and alert Englishman, who earned my master a great deal of money by his good work in carrying passengers from one island to another. Yet his sailors used to often get drunk and run away from his ship, which damaged his business. T

Captain Farmer took a liking to me. He often begged my master to let me go a trip with him as a sailor. Yet my master would tell him he could not spare me, even though the vessel sometimes could not sail as it hadn't enough crew. For there were very few sailors available on the island. In the end, my master reluctantly agreed to let sail with this captain. He warned the captain not to let me run away and said that he'd make the captain pay for me if I did. As a result, the captain kept a sharp eye on me whenever the ship anchored. As soon as we returned to Montserrat, I was sent for onshore again.

So was my slavery, sometimes I worked at one thing, and sometimes another. The captain and I were perhaps the most useful men in my master's employment. I soon became so useful to the captain that he used to often ask for me to go with him, even if it were for just a day to sail the nearby islands. When my master refused to let me go, the captain would swear and say he would not do the trip without me. He would tell my master that I was better than any three of the white men he had, as they used to behave badly, often getting drunk. When drunk, they would sometimes damage the boat, so she could not go to sea. My master knew this and, one day, to my great joy, he asked me whether I wanted to permanently stay aboard as a sailor. I was very happy at this, as I thought I might make a little money there, and that I might possibly make my escape. I also expected to get better food on the boat. I had often been very hungry ashore, even though my master treated his slaves unusually well. I, therefore, answered that I would go and be a sailor.

I was ordered on board straight away. However, when the ship was in port, I had no rest, as my master always wanted to have me with him. He was a very pleasant gentleman, I would not have thought of leaving him, if it weren't for my hopes of escape, or buying my freedom one day. The captain liked me very much, and I became his right-hand man. I did all I could to please him, and in return, I received better treatment from him than I believe any other slave in the West Indies ever did.

After I had been sailing for some time with the captain, I tried my luck as a merchant. I only had a half bit – which is three pence - to begin with. However, I trusted in God. On one of our trips to St. Eustatia, a Dutch island, I bought a glass tumbler with my half bit. When I came to Montserrat, I doubled my money by selling it for a bit, which is sixpence.

Luckily we made several trips to St. Eustatia, which was a big market in the West Indies, about 70 miles from Montserrat. On our next trip, I bought two more glass tumblers. When I came back, I sold them for two bits, which is equal to a shilling sterling. When we went again, I bought four more of these glasses, which I sold for four bits on our return to Montserrat. On our next voyage to St. Eustatia, I bought two glasses with one bit, and with the other three, I bought a three-pint jug of gin. When we returned to Montserrat, I sold the gin for eight bits, and the tumblers for two. My capital now amounted to a dollar. I had turned a half bit into ten bits in less than six weeks. I thanked the Lord that I was so rich.

As we sailed to different islands, I spent this money out on various things. I turned a good profit, especially when we went to Guadeloupe, Grenada, and other French islands. In this way, I went around the islands for over four years, always trading as I went. During this time, I was often treated badly. I also saw many wrongs done to other black people who dealt with Europeans. Even when we were dancing or making merry, they attacked and insulted us for no reason. More than once, I had to look up to God on high, as I had advised the poor fisherman sometime before.

I had not been long trading for myself, when the fisherman and I sailed together. He was urgently put on board our ship to work as crew on a voyage to Santa Cruz. He had brought all he had to trade, which was six bits' worth of limes and oranges in a bag. I had also my whole stock, which was about twelve bits' worth fruit in two bags, for we had heard that fruit sells well on Santa Cruz.

When we got there, he and I went ashore to sell our fruit. We had just landed when we were met by two white men, who took our three bags from us. We didn't know what they were going to do. For a while, we thought they were joking with us, but they soon let us know they were not. They took our bags to a nearby house which was next to the fort. We followed them all the way, begging them to give us back our fruit. They not only refused to return the bags, but swore at us, and threatened to flog us if we didn't leave. We told them these three bags were all we had in the world, and that we brought them to sell when we came from Montserrat, and pointed to our ship.

This went against us, as they now saw we were strangers as well as slaves. They swore, told us to be gone. They even took sticks to beat us, so we went off in the greatest confusion and despair. Just as I was about to make three times more profit than I ever had in any deal before, was I deprived of every penny I had.

We didn't know how to help ourselves. We went to the commanding officer of the fort and told him how we had been treated by these people. He answered our complaints with a volley of insults, and took a horse-whip to us. We left far faster than we came in. In the agony of this injustice, wished that God with his forked lightning would send these cruel oppressors to the dead.

We once again went back again to the house, and begged them again and again for our fruit until in the end, some others in the house asked if we would be happy if they kept one bag and gave us the other two. We agreed to this. They saw that the bag which belonged to my friend had both kinds of fruit and so they kept that. They gave back the other bags which were mine. As soon as I got them, I ran as fast as I could, and got the first black man I could to help me. My friend stayed a little longer to plead, telling them the bag they had was his, and was all he had in the world. This was no use, and he returned without it, crying for his loss. He then did look up to God on high, which so moved me with pity, that I gave him nearly one third of my fruit.

We then went to the markets to sell them. Fate was kinder to us than we could have expected, for we sold our fruit for a great price. I got about thirty-seven bits for my share. Such a surprising change of fortune in such little time seemed like a dream to me. This helped me learn to trust God in any situation.

After this, the captain took my side, and got me justice, when I was robbed or defrauded by these gentle Christian thieves. I often shuddered to hear endless blasphemy and swearing of such people, of all ages and classes.

On one of our trips to St. Kitt's I had eleven bits of my own. My friendly captain lent me five bits more, with which I bought a Bible. I was very glad to get this book, which I could hardly find anywhere. I think none were sold in Montserrat. When I was forced out of the Aetna, my Bible, and the Guide to the Indians - the two books I loved above all others - were left behind, to my sorrow.

While I was in St. Kitt's, a strange thing happened. A white man wanted to marry a free black woman, who had land and slaves in Montserrat. The clergyman told him it was against the law to marry a white and a black person in the church. The man then asked to be married on the water, which the parson agreed to. The two lovers went in one boat, and the parson in another. In this way, the wedding ceremony was performed. After this, the loving couple came on board our vessel, and my captain treated them very well. We brought them safely home to Montserrat.

It was frustrating to suffer new hardships each day, after having in the past tasted something of freedom and plenty. Every part of the world I had seen seemed a paradise when compared to the West Indies. My mind was always full thoughts of being free. Yet I wanted to gain my freedom honestly, as I always remembered the saying that honesty is the best policy. I also always followed the golden rule - to do unto others as I would want done to me.

However, I had been from childhood a firm believer in fate. I thought whatever fate in store must come to pass. I believed that if I were meant to be freed, nothing could stop this happening, even if it now seemed impossible. On the other hand, if it were my fate not to be freed, I would never be free, no matter what I tried.

With such thoughts, I prayed to God for my freedom. At the same time, I used every honest means to obtain it. In time, I had earned a few pounds, and was able to make more, which my friendly captain knew well. This sometimes caused him to try to get the better of me but, whenever he was annoyed at me, I used to tell him my mind. I said I would sooner die before I was mistreated as other black people were. I told him that my life would lose its relish, when my freedom was gone. I said this, even though I knew that my wellbeing and hopes of freedom in this world rested with this man.

Because he could not bear the thought of my not sailing with him, he always became kind after my threats. I, therefore, continued to work with him and, as I obeyed his orders and helped with his business, I gained his trust. I believed I would in the end gain my liberty through his kindness to me,

My life went on, filled with the thoughts of freedom. I resisted oppression as best I could. Yet my life was often at risk, especially when landing the boat in the surf, since I could not swim. The waves are extremely violent in the West Indies, and I was exposed to their rage and fury on all the islands. I have seen them strike and toss a boat right up an end, injuring many on board.

Once, on Grenada, when I and about eight others were rowing a large boat with two barrels of water in it, a wave struck us, and drove the boat and all in it ashore among some trees, above the high water mark. We had to get all the help we could from the nearest estate to mend the boat, and launch it again.

At Montserrat one night, when we were rowing hard off the shore, the boat capsized four times. The first time, I was very nearly drowned. However, the jacket I was wearing kept me above water for a few moments, while I called on a man near me who was a good swimmer, and told him I could not swim. He swam quickly to me, and caught hold of me, just as I was going under. He brought me into shallow water, and then went to get the boat too. As soon as we had got the water out of her, we tried to get through the surf three more times, for fear we would be in trouble for being late. On the fifth attempt, we broke through the waves, at the risk of our lives.

Another day, at bay in Montserrat, our captain and other three men were paddling in a large canoe to find rum and sugar, when a single wave tossed the canoe an amazing distance from the water. Some of us landed a stone's throw from each other. Most of us were very badly bruised. I often said that there was no place under heaven as this. I longed to leave it, and daily hoped that my master's promise of going to Philadelphia would come true.

While we lay at anchor in Montserrat, a cruel thing happened on board our ship, which filled me with horror.

114

I later learned that such practices were common. There was a very clever and decent free young mixed-race man who had sailed a long time with us. He had a free woman as his wife, with whom he had a child. She lived by the shore, and they were a happy family.

Our captain and mate, and all on board, knew that this young man had always been free since he was a child. No one had ever claimed him as their property. However, might often overcomes right in these parts. A captain from Bermuda, whose vessel had spent few days in the bay of Montserrat, came on board us. He saw the mixed race man, whose name was Joseph Clipson, and told him he was not free. He said that he had orders to bring him to Bermuda. The poor man did not believe that the captain was serious, but he soon saw he was. The captains' men laid violent hands on him. Although he showed a certificate proving he was born free in St. Kitt's, and most people on board knew he was free, he was forcibly taken from our ship.

He then asked to be taken before the magistrates ashore, and these thieves of human rights promised him they would do this. But instead of that, they took him on board their ship. The next day, they took him away, without giving him a hearing on shore, or letting him see his wife or child – who he was probably doomed to never again see in this world. This was not the only time I saw such barbarity.

In Jamaica and on the other islands, I often saw free men I had known in America taken into bondage. I have heard similar stories even in Philadelphia. Were it not for the kindness of the Quakers in that city, many of the black race, who breathe the air of liberty, would be groaning under some planter's chains.

These experiences opened my mind to a new awareness. I had before thought only slavery dreadful. Now, the state of the free black people seemed as bad, and in some ways worse - as they live in daily fear of losing their liberty. They are routinely insulted and robbed, without hope of justice. For the West Indian laws don't allow a free black man's evidence to be heard in court.

It is hardly surprising that slaves, who are reasonably treated, prefer even the misery of slavery to this mockery of freedom. I now became completely disgusted with the West Indies. I knew that I would never be free until I left those islands.

I became determined to try everything I could to become free and to return to Old England. I thought that learning navigation might be of use to me. I did not intend to run away unless I was ill-treated. Yet, if that happened, and I understood navigation, I might be able to escape in our sloop, which was one of the swiftest sailing vessels in the West Indies. I would have plenty of crew to join me if I tried to escape by sailing for England.

I agreed to pay the mate of our ship 24 dollars to teach me navigation. I had paid him part of the money when the captain learned of this. He gave out to the mate for taking payment from me for this. However, my progress in the art of navigation was slowed by the demands of our work. Had I wished to run away, I had plenty of chances to do so. For example, when we were at the island of Guadeloupe, there was a large fleet of merchant ships bound for France. Seamen were very scarce, and they offered from fifteen to twenty pounds for crew for the voyage.

Our mate, and all the white sailors, left our vessel for these wages, and went on board of the French ships. They asked me to go with them, for they liked me and knew I could sail well. They swore to protect me, if I would go. As the fleet was to sail the next day, I believe I could have made it safely to Europe with them. However, as my master was kind, I did not want to try to leave him. I again remembered the old saying, that "honesty is the best policy," and so I left them to go without me.

My captain was very afraid that I would leave him at that time. Yet my faithfulness to my master ended up working out well for me later on. My faithfulness caused the captain to trust me so much that he began to teach me navigation himself. Yet some of our passengers, and others, saw this and said it was a very dangerous thing to let a black man know navigation. This meant I was again held back in my learning. At the end of 1764, my master bought a larger sloop, called the Providence, which was about seventy or eighty tons. I went with the captain into this vessel, and we got ready to take a load of new slaves for Georgia and Charles Town.

My master left me entirely to the captain, though he still wished for me to be with him. As I wished to lose sight of the West Indies, I was always happy to sail to another country. I got ready all the goods I could to trade and, when the vessel was ready, we sailed for America, to my great joy.

When we got to Georgia and Charles Town, I thought I would have an opportunity to sell my small few goods for profit. However, particularly in Charles Town, I once again met with white buyers who treated me unfairly, as they had in other places. Despite this, I remained determined. We soon loaded the ship again, and we returned to Montserrat. We then sailed amongst the rest of the islands, where I sold my goods well. In this way, I continued trading during the year 1764, despite suffering the usual harassment.

In 1765, my master made his vessel ready for a voyage to Philadelphia. When we were loading her, and getting ready for the voyage, I worked at the double. I hoped I would get enough money through these voyages to buy my freedom, if that should please God. I also hoped to see the town of Philadelphia, which I had heard a great deal about for years. Besides, I had always seen my master's promise fulfilled.

One Sunday, I was in the midst of such thoughts, while busy getting my merchandise ready for the voyage, when my master sent for me. I went to his house, where I found my master and the captain together. I was astonished when he told me he heard I was going to run away from him when I got to Philadelphia. "Therefore," he said, "I must sell you again. You cost me a great deal of money, no less than forty pounds sterling. It will not do to lose so much. You are a valuable fellow and I can get one hundred guineas, for you any day from many gentlemen in this island."

Then he told me of Captain Doran's brother-in-law, who was a severe master He wanted to buy me to make me his overseer. My captain also said he could get much more than a hundred guineas for me in Carolina. This I knew to be a fact, for the Carolina gentleman who wanted to buy me had come on board our ship several times. He had asked me to live with him, saying he would treat me well. When I asked what work he would have me do, he said that since I was a sailor, he would make me a captain of one of his rice vessels. I refused, fearing that he might mean to sell me.

I told the gentleman I would not live with him on any condition, and that I certainly would run away with his rice vessel. He said he did not fear that, as he would catch me again. Then he told me how cruelly he would treat me if I ran away. My captain, let him know that I knew something about navigation, so he thought better of it and, to my great joy, he went away.

I now told my master I did not say I would run away in Philadelphia. I told him I did not plan to run, as neither he nor the captain treated did not treated me badly. If they did, I certainly would have tried to run before now. I said I thought that if it were God's will I should be freed, it would be so; but if it was not his will, it would not happen. I said hoped that if I were freed, it would be by honest means.

I knew my master could do as he pleased, while I could only hope and trust in God. Yet at that moment, my mind became filled with plans to escape. I then asked the captain whether he ever saw any sign of my making the least attempt to run away. I asked him if I did not always come on board at the time I should. I reminded him that, when all our men left us at Guadeloupe and went on board of the French fleet, they asked me to go with them. I asked whether he could not have got me again had I done so.

To my great surprise, and even greater joy, the captain confirmed everything I said and more. He said he had watched to see if I would try to escape both at St. Eustatia and in America, and he never found that I made the slightest effort to run. On the contrary, I always came on board according to his orders. He said he believed that if I ever meant to run away, I could have done so the night that all the crew left our ship at Guadeloupe.

It turned out that the mate had lied to my master. The captain then told my master that the reason the mate had done this. It was because I told the captain about the provisions the mate had stolen from our ship.

The captain's words, were like life to the dead to me. Instantly, my soul soared. It flew higher when I heard my master say that I was a sensible fellow, and he never really intended to sell me. He said that, but for captain's words, he would keep me working the stores about as I had done before. He also thought that by trading little things in ports, I might make money. He also said he would encourage me in trade by lending me half a barrel of rum and half a hogshead of sugar at a time so that I might earn money enough to purchase my freedom. He said that, when that happened, he would let me have my freedom for forty pounds sterling, which was the same price he paid for me.

This gladdened my heart beyond measure. This was what I had believed my master to be like for a long time. I immediately said to him, "Sir, I always had that very thought of you, indeed I had, and that made me so diligent in serving you."

He then gave me the largest silver coin I had ever seen, and told me to get ready for the voyage. He said he would lend me a cask of sugar and one of rum. He also said he had two kindly sisters in Philadelphia, who might give me some useful things.

Then, my noble captain told me to go aboard. Knowing how Africans like to talk, he ordered me not to say anything of this matter to anybody. He promised that the lying mate would not sail with us anymore. This was a change indeed. In that single hour, I had felt the most cutting pain, and the fullest joy. It caused feelings in me that I was could only express in my face. My heart was so grateful, that I could have kissed both of their feet. When I left the room, I flew to the ship which was being loaded. My master, true to his word, trusted me with a cask of rum, and another of sugar.

We sailed safely to the elegant town of Philadelphia. I soon sold my goods at a good price and in this charming place, I found everything plentiful and cheap.

While I was in Philadelphia, an extraordinary thing happened to me. I had been told one evening of a *wise* woman called Mrs. Davis, who revealed secrets and foretold the future. I put little faith in this story at first, as I could not believe that any mortal could foresee the workings of fate. Nor did I believe in any other revelation than that of the Holy Scriptures. However, I was astonished to meet this woman in a dream that night - even though I had never before seen her in my life. This made such an impression on me, that I could not get the idea of seeing her out of my mind.

That the evening, after we finished work, I asked where she lived. I was directed to her and, to my surprise, saw the same woman as I had seen in my vision. She was even wearing the very same dress as when appeared to me to wear in the vision. She immediately told me that she knew

I had dreamed of her the night before. She then told me many things that had happened in my life, with an accuracy that astonished me. She finally told me that I would not be long a slave. This was the best news I had ever heard. I believed it too, as she had so accurately told of past events in my life.

She said I would be in danger of my life twice in the next eighteen months. She said that, if I escaped these dangers, all would be well. She gave me her blessing, and we parted. We stayed some time in Philadelphia, until our vessel was loaded. We sailed from this lovely place for Montserrat, once more to meet the raging surf.

We arrived safe at Montserrat, where we discharged our cargo. Soon after, we took slaves on board for St. Eustatia. From there, we sailed to Georgia. I had always worked hard, to make our voyages as short as possible. From over-working myself in this way in Georgia, I caught a fever. I was very ill for eleven days and near death. Eternity was impressed on my mind, and I feared the awful moment of death. I prayed to God to spare me, promising him that I would be good, if recovered. After a time, a well-known doctor saw me, and I recovered my health.

Soon after, we loaded the ship and sailed for Montserrat. During the passage, since my health was restored, I had plenty work to do on board the ship. Yet, as we sailed on, my desire to keep my promise to God began to fail. As we drew nearer to the islands, it was as if the very air became fatal to goodness.

After we arrived at Montserrat, I went ashore, where I forgot my promise to God to be good if he spared me. Sadly, our heart often leaves the God it wishes to love. How the things of this world captivate our senses, and our souls.

After our ship was unloaded, we took in, as usual, some of the poor oppressed natives of Africa and other black people. We then set off again for Georgia and Charlestown. We arrived at Georgia, and landed some of the slaves, before proceeding to Charlestown with the rest. While we were there, I saw the town lit up in celebration. The guns were fired, and bonfires were lit to celebrate the repeal of the stamp act.

Here I sold off some goods. The white men bought them with smooth promises and fine words, but gave me poor payment. There was one man who bought a cask of rum from me, but wouldn't pay me for it, despite my captain's efforts. Being a black man, I could not make him pay me. This troubled me and I had to skip worship on Sunday to find this man. I hired some black men to row me across the water, where I found him. After much argument, he, at last, paid me in dollars but some of them were copper and so of no value. He took advantage of my being a black man, and told me to put up with those or have nothing.

Immediately afterwards, I was trying to use these copper dollars in the market, when other white men abused me for trying to pass bad coin. Although I showed them the man who gave me these coins, I was, in one minute, tied up and flogged - without either judge or jury. I ran off, and so escaped the foot-whipping was also to receive. I got on board as fast as I could. I was in fear of these men until we sailed, which we thankfully did soon after.

We soon came to Georgia, where we were to complete our loading. Here an even worse fate awaited me. One Sunday night, I was with some black people in their master's yard in Savannah. These were slaves of Doctor Perkins, who was a very severe and cruel man, Dr Perkins came in drunk and was unhappy to see a strange black man in his yard. He and a ruffian of a white servant of his, attacked me instantly. Both of them struck me with the first weapons they could get hold of. I cried out as long as I could for help and mercy. Although I explained my situation, and even though he knew my captain, it was no use. They beat and mangled me, leaving me near dead. I lost so much blood from the wounds I received, that I lay motionless. I was so numbed that I could not feel anything for many hours. Early in the morning, they took me away to the jail.

As I did not return to the ship all night, my captain, became uneasy and asked after me. When he found out where I was, immediately came to me. As soon as the good man saw me so cut and mangled, he could not help weeping. He soon got me out of jail, and to his lodgings. He immediately sent for the best doctors in the town, who at first declared that I would not recover.

My captain then went to all the lawyers in the town for their advice, but they told him they could do nothing for me, as I was a black man. He then went to Doctor Perkins, the hero who had vanquished me, and threatened him, swearing he would take his revenge, and challenged him to fight. But cowardice is always the companion of cruelty, and the Doctor refused.

However, by the skilfulness of one Doctor Brady, I at last began to slowly recover. Although I was so sore with the wounds I had all over me, I could not rest in any posture. Yet the captain's worries about me caused me pain too. That good man nursed me and watched me through the night. Thanks to his care, and that of the doctor, I was able to get out of bed in about sixteen or eighteen days.

All this time, I was needed on board, as I used to often go up and down the river for rafts, and other parts of our cargo, and stow them when the mate was sick or absent. After about four weeks I was able to go back on duty. A fortnight after that, we had got in all our cargo and our vessel set sail for Montserrat. After a voyage of three weeks we arrived there safely, towards the end of the year. So ended my adventures in 1764. for I did not leave Montserrat again until the beginning of the following year.

CHAPTER 7

THE PRICE OF FREEDOM

Each day brought me nearer my freedom. I was keen to go to sea, so I could gather enough money to buy my liberty. In early 1766, my master bought another sloop, named Nancy. She was the largest single-masted sloop I had ever seen. My captain had the choice of three ships, and I was glad he chose the largest. For in a larger vessel, I would have more room to carry goods to sell.

When we had sold our old vessel, and loaded the Nancy, I took in as large a cargo as I could, trusting God to bless my efforts. I had made almost three hundred per cent profit on the four barrels of pork I brought from Charlestown, and could afford plenty of goods.

On our passage to Philadelphia, as we drew near the land, I surprised to see some whales. I had never seen such large sea creatures before. As we sailed past the land one morning, I saw a whale calf close to the ship. It was about the length of a small boat, and it followed us all day, until we went inside the capes.

We arrived safe and in good time at Philadelphia, where I sold most of my goods to the Quakers. They seemed to be a very honest sort of people. They never attempted to trick me. I, therefore, liked them, and from then on I preferred to deal with above all others.

One Sunday morning while I was going to church in Philadelphia, I happened to pass a Quaker meeting house. The doors were open, and the house was full of people. I was curious to go inside. I went in and was surprised to see a tall woman standing in centre of the hall, speaking words which I could not understand. I had never seen anything like this before. I stood and stared in wonder for some time.

I later asked what that woman had said, but nobody would tell me, so I left. Soon after, I came to a church crowded with people. The churchyard was also full, and some people were even standing on ladders, looking in the windows. I thought this strange, as in England or the West Indies I had never seen churches so crowded. I asked what this meant, and was told the famous Rev. Mr. George Whitfield was preaching.

I had often heard of this gentleman, and had long wished to hear him, so I pressed in amongst the crowd. When I got into the church I saw a preacher who was sincerely encouraging the people to live better. He was sweating as much I ever did in slavery on Montserrat beach. I was impressed with this, as I had never seen a preacher exert himself like this. I now understood why those who didn't had small congregations.

When we had loaded our cargo in Philadelphia, we left this fruitful land once more and set sail for Montserrat. My business had gone so well that I thought I might make enough from selling my goods when we arrived at Montserrat to purchase my freedom. Sadly, as soon as our vessel arrived, my master came on board and ordered us to sail to St. Eustatia to discharge our cargo there. From there, we were to sail for Georgia. I was disappointed but I accepted my fate, and sailed went to St. Eustatia. After we had discharged our cargo, we took on board livestock and slaves. Here I sold some of my goods fairly well. Yet I kept some money, as I could not buy goods as profitably there as on other islands.

We sailed for Georgia. I was glad to get there, though I had good reason to dislike the place after my last experience in Savannah. I longed to get back to Montserrat and to buy my freedom. As soon as we arrived in Savannah, I met the good Dr Brady and thanked him for his kindness.

While we were in Savannah, an odd thing happened to the captain and me. A silversmith, whom we had brought to Georgia a few years before, arranged to return with us to the West Indies, promising the Captain a great deal of money. We thought he was rich, and he seemed to like the captain. While we loaded our ship, he man was taken ill soon became very unwell. The sicker he got, the more spoke of giving the captain what he had promised. The captain expected a considerable gift upon the death of this man, who had no wife or child. He looked after him day and night. I used also to go with the captain to care for him. The captain promised me ten pounds for my trouble, when he got the man's property. I thought this would be great, although I be then almost had enough money to purchase my freedom.

Expecting this extra money, I spent eight pounds on a suit of fine clothes to dance in upon the day I gained my freedom, which I hoped come very soon. We continued to look after this man, until he died. After we were sent to bed the night he died, about two o'clock in the morning, the captain was sent for and was told the man was dead. The captain then came to my bed, woke me, and told me the news. He asked me to get a lamp, and come with him. I told him I was very sleepy, and wished he would take somebody else. I said that, as the man was dead, he needed no more help, and things could until the morning. "No, no," said the captain, "we will have the money tonight, I cannot wait till tomorrow, so let us go."

I got up and lit a lamp, and away we both went. We saw the man, as dead as could be. The Captain said he would give him a grand burial, in thanks for the promised treasure. He asked that all the dead man's belongings be brought out. There was a nest of trunks which he had been given the keys to, when the man was ill. We opened them eagerly. There were a smaller one within each one, and we impatiently unlocked them, At last, we came to the smallest, and opening it, we saw it was full of papers.

We thought these were banknotes, and our hearts leapt for joy and the captain, clapped his hands and cried out, "Thank God, here it is." But, when we examined the supposed treasure, we found it was an empty nothing. The whole amount in the nest of trunks was only a dollar and a half. All that the man possessed would not pay for his coffin. We went away and left the deceased to do as well as he could for himself. We had taken good care of him for nothing.

We set sail once more for Montserrat, and arrived there safely, but unhappy with our friend the silversmith. When we had unloaded the ship, and I had sold my trading goods, I found myself with forty-seven pounds. I asked my true friend, the captain, how I offer my master the money for my freedom. He told me to come when he and my master would be having breakfast together. That morning, I went and met the Captain at my master' house, as he had arranged.

I went in and greeted my master, with my money in my hand, and many fears in my heart. I asked him to be true to his offer to allow me buy my freedom for forty pounds. My question seemed to confuse him and he began to recoil. My heart sank within me. "What," he asked, "give you your freedom? Why, where did you get the money? Have you got forty pounds sterling?" "Yes, sir," I answered. "How did you get it?" he asked. I told him, very honestly, about my trade.

The captain said that he knew I got the money honestly and with hard work and thrift. My master replied that I got money much faster than he did and said he would not have made me the promise he did, if he had thought I should have got money so soon.

"Come, come," said the captain, clapping my master on the back, "Come, Robert, I think you must let him have his freedom. You have spent your money very well. You have received good interest for it all this time, and here is now the principal at last. I know Gustavus has earned you more than a hundred a year, and he will still save you money, as he will not leave you. Come, Robert, take the money."

My master then said he would not break than his promise and, taking the money, he told me to go to the Secretary at the Register Office, and get my manumission drawn up, as this document would prove I was a free man.

These words of my master were like a voice from heaven to me. All my fears were turned into bliss. I bowed with gratitude, unable to express my feelings, but by my overflowing eyes. My true and worthy friend, the captain, congratulated us both with a full heart.

I was transported by joy and I had thanked these worthy friends as best I could. I rose with a heart full of love, and left the room, to go to the Register Office. As left the house, I remembered the psalm, "I glorified God in my heart, in whom I trusted." These words had been burned in my mind, since the day I was enslaved a second time. I now saw them fulfilled.

As I flew to the Register Office I could hardly believe I was not dreaming. This feeling was more than the joy of a conquering hero, or the tender mother who has just found her long lost baby. It was more than the feelings of the hungry sailor, at the sight of a safe and friendly port.

My feet were winged with joy, and I told everyone I met of my happiness. I cried of the goodness of my master and captain. When I got to the office and told the Registrar my news, he congratulated me, and said he would write up my manumission document for half price, which was a guinea. I thanked him for his kindness. I took the document and rushed to my master for him to sign it, so I would be released. He signed the manumission that day. I had been a slave that morning, trembling at the will of another, but by nightfall, I was my own master, completely free.

I thought this the happiest of my life. My joy was shared by the blessings and prayers of the black people of the island, particularly the old, who were close to my heart.

Because my manumission document has something strange to it, and shows the power and dominion one man can claim over another, I shall share it with you:

Montserrat.—To all men unto whom these presents shall come: I Robert King, of the parish of St. Anthony in the said island, merchant, send greeting: Know ye, that I the aforesaid Robert King, for and in consideration of the sum of seventy pounds current money of the said island, to me in hand paid, and to the intent that a negro man-slave, named Gustavus Vassa, shall and may become free, have manumitted, emancipated, enfranchised, and set free, and by these presents do manumit, emancipate, enfranchise, and set free, the aforesaid negro man-slave, named Gustavus Vassa, for ever, hereby giving, granting, and releasing unto him, the said Gustavus Vassa, all right, title, dominion, sovereignty, and property, which, as lord and master over the aforesaid Gustavus Vassa, I had, or now I have, or by any means whatsoever I may or can hereafter possibly have over him the aforesaid negro, for ever. In witness whereof I the abovesaid Robert King have unto these presents set my hand and seal, this tenth day of July, in the year of our Lord one thousand seven hundred and sixty-six.

Robert King.

Signed, sealed, and delivered in the presence of Terrylegay Montserrat.

Registered the within manumission at full length, this eleventh day of July, 1766, in liber D.

Terrylegay, Register.

The fair and black people of the island now gave me a new name. To me, this was the best name in the world:

Freeman. At the dances I held to celebrate, I cut a dashing figure, in my fine blue Georgia clothes, I thought. Some of the black women, who once were cold, now seemed far more friendly. Yet my heart was still fixed on London, where I hoped to go before long.

My captain and my former master heard that I was thinking of London. They said to me, "We hope you won't leave us, but that you'll stay with the ships." My feelings struggled between desire and duty, but gratitude got the better of me. Despite my wish to be in London, I said I would go in the ships. From that day, I was hired as an able-bodied sailor, on thirty-six shillings per month, along with what I could make from trade.

My plan was to make a voyage or two, to please my master and the captain. I decided that the following year, if God wished it, I would see old England once more. I thought I might surprise my old master, Captain Pascal, who was often on my mind. I still loved him, despite how he had treated me. I enjoyed imagining what he would say when he saw what God had done for me in so short a time. I was now a free man, instead of being under the cruel yoke of some planter, as he might think. I often entertained myself with such daydreams, to shorten the time until my return to London.

I was once again in my original, free, African state. I went on board the Nancy, after having got all things ready for the voyage. In this state of serenity, I sailed for St. Eustatia. Smooth seas and calm weather meant we soon arrived there. We took our cargo on board, and proceeded to Savannah, Georgia in August, 1766.

While in Georgia, I took my usual boat trips up the river for cargo. On these journeys, I was often attacked by alligators, which were numerous on that coast. I shot many of them when they tried to get into our boats. I became very frightened of them. I once saw a young one sold alive in Georgia for six pence.

During our stay in Savannah, one evening a slave belonging to a local merchant of Savannah, came near our ship. He began to insult me. I asked him to stop, with as much patience as I had, as I knew there was no law for a free black man in Georgia. Instead of taking my advice, he went on insulting me, and even struck me. At this, I lost all temper, and I fell on him and beat him soundly.

The next morning, his master came to our ship as we lay alongside the wharf, and told me to come ashore so he might have me flogged all around the town, for beating his black slave. I told him he had insulted me, and had provoked me, by first striking me.

I had already told my captain about the whole incident that morning and asked him to go with me to Mr. Read, to help avoid trouble. He said that it didn't matter, and if Mr. Read said anything, he would sort it out. He asked me to instead go to work, which I did. The Captain was on board when Mr. Read came and he told him I was now a free man.

When Mr. Read told to him to deliver me up to him regardless, I became more frightened. I thought I'd better stay where I was and avoid going ashore where I would be flogged around the town, without judge or jury. I therefore refused to stir. Mr. Read went away, swearing he would bring all the constables in the town to get me out of the ship.

When he was gone, I thought his threat might prove true. I had seen free black people treated badly many times. Just a short time before then, in Savannah, there was a free black man, a carpenter, who I knew. He asked a gentleman for wages he had earned, and was put into gaol. He was later sent from Georgia, thanks to false rumours that he planned to set fire to the gentleman's house, and run away with his slaves. I was therefore very worried about getting a flogging.

I dreaded the thought of being flogged and striped. A rage seized my soul, I said I'd to resist the first man to try to lay hands on me or punish me without a trial. I said I'd sooner die like a free man than allow myself to be whipped by ruffians, and have my blood drawn like a slave.

The captain and crew were more cautious. They advised me to quickly hide myself. They said Mr. Read was a very spiteful man, and that he would soon come on board with constables to take me. At first I refused to take their advice, as I wanted to stand my ground. In the end, I listened to the pleas of the captain and Mr. Dixon, with whom he stayed in Savannah. I went to hide at Mr. Dixon's house, which was a little out of town, at a place called Yeamachra.

I had just left, when Mr. Read and the constables came for me, and searched the ship. When they didn't find me there, Mr Read swore he'd have me dead or alive. I was hidden for about five days. Some of the captain's friends told him that he should not allow me to be threatened unjustly. They said they would get me on board another ship. My captain went to Mr. Read and said he needed me to manage the loading of the ship, and that my absence would hurt its owner financially. He asked him to forgive me, as he said he never had a complaint about me before, in all the years I had been with him.

Mr. Read said I could go to hell, but that he would leave me be. My captain came to tell me that all was well, and asked me to go on board. Some of my friends then asked if he had got the police warrant from them, but the captain said he hadn't. My friends said I should stay in the house and that they would get me aboard some other vessel before the evening.

When the captain heard this, he became upset. He immediately went to the police for the warrant and persuaded my hunters to give it to him. Although I had to pay the expenses. I thanked all my friends for their help and went on board again to find plenty of work to be done, for we were in a rush to finish loading the ship. We were to carry twenty cattle with us to the West Indies, where they can fetch a fine price.

In order to encourage me to work fast, to make up for the time we had lost, the captain promised me that I could bring two bullocks of my own with me to Montserrat. This made me work even harder. As soon as I had got the vessel loaded while doing the mate's work as well as my own, I asked the captain if I could bring my two bullocks on board but, to my great surprise, he now said me there was no room for them. I then asked if I could take one, but he said he could not. I was angry at this, and told him I couldn't believe what he was saying, and that I couldn't think well of any man so untrue to his word.

We argued, and I let him know that I planned to leave the ship. He then seemed very put out. Our mate, who had been very sick, advised him to ask me to stay. The captain then spoke very kindly to me, making many promises and saying that, as the mate was so sickly, he couldn't do without me. He said that, as the safety of the ship and its cargo depended so much upon me, he hoped that I would forgive him, and swore he would make it all up to me we arrived in the West Indies. Hearing all this, I agreed to slave on as before.

Soon after, as the bullocks were coming on board, one of them ran at the captain, and butted him so furiously in the chest, that he never recovered from the blow. In order to make up for his broken promise about the bullocks, the captain begged me to take some turkeys and other birds with me, He said I could take as many as I could find room for. I told him that he knew well I had never carried any turkeys before, as I thought they were too fragile to cross the seas. Yet he continued to beg me to buy them and the more I argued against it, the more he asked me to take them, He even agreed to insure me against any losses that might happen to them. I agree to take them, but I thought this very strange, as he had never acted in this way before. In the end I took four dozen turkeys.

I was so unhappy with what had happened, that I decided to make no more voyages to this place, nor with this captain. I began to worry that my first voyage as a free man would be the worst I ever made.

As we set sail for Montserrat, the captain and the mate were both complaining of sickness. As we sailed on, they worse. This was about November, and we were not long at sea before we met with strong northerly gales and rough seas. After seven or eight days, all the bullocks were nearly drowned, and four or five of them died.

Our ship had never been watertight, but it became much worse now. Although there were only 9 crew on board, we had to man the pumps every half hour. The captain and mate came on deck as often as they were able, but this was seldom. They became sicker so fast, and could only make observations of the sun to navigate the ship more a few times.

Running the ship soon rested completely upon me. I had to navigate her as best I could. I had to try to recall the correct direction to sail, since I could not work a sextant. The captain was now very sorry he had not taught me navigation, and swore he would if he ever got well again. After about seventeen days at sea, his illness became so bad, that he couldn't leave his bed. He stayed alert until the end, as this fair and kind man was very concerned about the ship. When this good friend felt death approaching, he called me by my name. When I came to him, he asked - with almost his last breath - if he had ever done me any harm?

"God forbid I should think so," I replied, saying if he had, I wouldn't be in such sorrow by his bedside. He died without saying another word. The next day, we sent his body to the deep. Every man on board loved this man, and was sad at his death, but I was deeply affected by it. I did not know the strength of my feeling for him until he was gone.

I had every reason in the world to be fond of him. As well as he being friendly, generous, kind and fair, he was to me a friend and a father. Had he died just five months before, I believe I wouldn't have obtained my freedom when I did - and I might never have.

After the captain died, the mate came on deck and made observations as best he could, but it was no use. After a few days, the last few bullocks died. The turkeys I had did well, even though they were kept on the deck, exposed to so wet and bad weather. I later made a profit of almost three hundred per cent on them. It turned out that I was lucky not to have bought the bullocks, as they would have died with the rest. I could not help seeing this small thing as the work of God, and so I was thankful.

Looking after the ship took up all my time and attention. As we had entered the trade winds, I thought we would soon come upon the islands. I steered right for Antigua, as it was the nearest island to us. After nine or ten days, we made this island, to our great joy.

The next day, we arrived safely in Montserrat. Many people there were surprised to hear about me sailing the sloop into port. I was now given the nickname of Captain. This pleased me, as I was happy to have as high a title as any free man on the island. When the death of my captain became known, he was mourned by all who knew him.

At the same time, the black captain's success caused the affection of my friends to grow.

Chapter 8

Shipwreck

The death of my captain meant that I had lost my great protector and friend. I had little reason to stay in the West Indies, except my gratitude to my old master, Mr. King. I thought I had shown him thanks enough by bringing his ship and cargo home safely. I began to think of leaving this part of the world, which I had grown so tired of. I dreamt again of returning to England, where my heart had always been. Yet Mr. King begged me to stay with his ship. As he had done so much for me, I found myself unable to refuse.

I agreed to sail once again to Georgia, as the mate was so ill that he was fairly useless about the ship. A new captain named William Phillips was found. I had known him long before. After we had refitted our vessel, and taken some slaves on board, we set sail for St. Eustatia. We stayed there for a few days and on the 30th of January 1767, we sailed for Georgia.

Our new captain boasted of his skill in navigating a vessel. He steered a new course, for Georgia more to the west than we had sailed before. This seemed very strange to me.

On the fourth of February, as we sailed our new course, I dreamt the ship was wrecked amid surf and rocks, and that I had to save everyone on board. The next night, I dreamed the very same dream. These dreams had little impact on my mind at the time.

The next evening, just after eight o'clock I was down below pumping the vessel. I was weary after all my work that day, and angry at the ship leaking so much, and I swore, "Damn the ship's bottom out." At once, I felt guilty for swearing in this way.

That night, I had barely fallen asleep when I dreamed the same dream again about the ship being wrecked. At twelve o'clock, it was my watch and so I went on deck. At half past one in the morning, the man at the helm saw something under the water that the sea broke against. He shouted to me that there was a grampus, and called me to look at it. I went and watched it for some time but, when I saw the sea break against it again and again, I said it was not a fish but a rock.

I rushed to the captain, and told him the danger we were in, and asked him to come on deck. He said he would, so I went on deck again. But at soon as I went on deck, the wind calmed a little, and the current began to bring the ship sideways towards the rocks. Yet the captain did not appear, so I went to him again. I told him the vessel was near a large rock, and begged him to hurry. He said he would, and I returned to the deck. I now saw we were less than a pistol shot from the rocks, and I heard the noise of the breakers all around us. I was terrified at this, and I ran down to the captain again, asking him why he did not come up, and what he meant by all this? I cried, "The breakers are all around us, and the ship is almost on the rocks." With that, he came on deck with me, and we tried to put the ship about, to get her out of the current. However, it was no use, as the wind was too light.

We called all hands on deck and we soon tied a large rope to the anchor. By this time, the surf was foaming all around us, making a dreadful noise as it broke. The very moment we dropped our anchor, the ship struck against the rocks. One swell now followed another rapidly, and the roaring of the waves increased until, with one huge heave of the waves, the sloop was broken open and became stuck on the rocks.

I had never seen such a scene of horror before. All my sins stared me in the face. I thought that God was avenging me for cursing the very ship that my life depended on. My spirits fell, and I thought I'd go to the bottom at any moment. I promised that if I were saved, I would never swear again. As the dreadful surf thundered with unremitting fury among the rocks, I remembered God, even though I feared that I did not deserve to be forgiven. Yet I hoped that since he had often protected me before, he might do so again. I remembered the many mercies he had shown me in the past. This gave me some small hope that he might still help me.

I then began to think how we might survive. My mind became full of plans and confused schemes. Yet I knew not how we might escape death. The captain ordered the hatches to be nailed down on the slaves in the hold. There were more than twenty slaves below, all of whom would have died, if the captain was obeyed.

When he asked the man to nail down the hatches, I believed my sin in cursing the ship was the cause of this. I thought that God would charge me with these people's blood. This terrible thought rushed upon my mind with such violence, that it overpowered me and I fainted.

I awoke just as the crew were about to nail down the hatches. Seeing this, I begged them to stop. The captain then said it must be done. I asked why. He said that the slaves would try to get into the small boat, and we would all be drowned as it could carry ten people at most.

I could no longer restrain my emotions. I told him he deserved drowning for not knowing how to navigate the vessel. I believe the crew would have thrown him overboard then, if I had given the least hint of the idea. However, the hatches were not nailed down. After all, none of us could leave the ship as it was so dark, and we didn't know which way to go. We also thought that the small boat would not survive the surf, so we agreed to stay on part of the ship that was still above the water, and to trust God until daylight came.

I said we should get the small boat prepared for morning, and some of us set about it. Others stopped caring for the ship or themselves, and began drinking. Our small boat had a hole nearly two feet long in her bottom, and we had nothing to mend her with. However, necessity being the mother of invention, I took some leather and nailed it over the hole, and plastered the patch with grease.

We then watched anxiously for daylight. Every minute seemed an hour until dawn came. At last, morning greeted our longing eyes. At the same time, we were happy to see the swell grow calmer. The next thing we saw to raise our spirits, was a small island, about five or six miles off. Our happiness at seeing the island was short lived, as dawn then revealed a shallow reef blocking our passage to the island.

There was no choice but to try to cross the shallow reef. We put a few people in the boat at once so that the boat would float higher in the water. As we rowed over the shallow reef, we often had to get out to drag and lift the boat across the coral. Our legs became cut and torn from the rocks by this tiring work. Only four men would pull with me at the oars. These were three black men and a Dutch creole sailor.

We rowed from the ship to the island five times that day, but no others helped us. Had we not done this, I believe the ship's people would have drowned. Not one of the white men did anything to save their lives. Indeed, they soon got so drunk that they were only able to lay about on the deck like pigs. In the end, we had to lift them into the boat and carry them ashore by force. The lack of any help made our work unbearably hard. I rowed so much that day that the skin was entirely stripped from my hands.

We toiled all day until we had brought everyone on board safely to the shore. Out of the thirty-two people on board, we lost not a soul. My dream now returned to my mind with all its force. Every part of it had come true. The shipwreck was just as I had dreamt and I could not help looking on myself as being mainly responsible for saving our people. Because some of our crew got drunk, the rest of us had to double our efforts. It was lucky we did because, before long, the patch of leather on the boat would have given way, and she would have sunk.

Who could think that men should be so careless of the danger they were in? If the wind had come up after the ship went aground, we would have lost all hope of being saved. Even though I warned the crew who were drinking, and begged them to work to save us all, they went on drinking, as they had lost the faintest spark of reason. I could not help thinking, that if any of these people had been lost, God would charge me with their lives. Perhaps this thought caused me to work so hard to save everyone. Afterwards, the people all seemed to know what I had done for them. While we were on the island, I was treated as their leader.

I brought limes, oranges and lemons ashore and, seeing that the soil was good, I planted a number of them to help anyone that might be cast away here in future.

We later learned that this was one of the Bahama islands, which are a cluster of large islands, with smaller ones - called keys - scattered amongst them. Our island was about a mile around, with a white sandy beach running along its shore.

As we went to land on the island, we saw were some large birds, called flamingos, in the reflection of the low sun. As they walked about, they looked as large as men and we could not make out what they were. Our captain swore they were cannibals. This created a panic among the crew and we decided what to do. The captain wanted to go to another island that we could see a great way off. I was against this idea, as it would mean we would not be able to save all the people still aboard. I said, "let us go ashore here, as the cannibals may run from us." We then we steered towards them and, as we came nearer, to our joy and wonder, they walked away from us, and soon took flight, which relieved us of our fears.

The island had so many turtles and fish that we caught them without bait. The fish tasted sublime after the dry, salted provisions we had aboard. There was also a large rock on the beach, about ten feet high, shaped like a bowl. We could not help but think that God had made this rock to give us water. Yet if we did not drink this water soon after it rained, it became as salty as sea-water.

After we had eaten and drank, our first task was to make tents for shelter. We built these as best we could with sails we had brought from the ship. We then began to think how we might get off this uninhabited island. We decided to repair our boat, so we could put to sea to find a ship or an inhabited island. It took us eleven days to repair the boat get ready for sea, with a sail and other necessary items.

Once all was ready, the captain asked me to stay on shore while he went to sea seeking a ship to take all the people off the island. I refused to stay and so the captain and myself, with five crew, set off in the boat towards New Providence. We only had two musket loads of gunpowder with us, if we should be attacked. As provisions, we had three gallons of rum, four gallons of water, some salt beef and biscuits.

With these few things, we set out to sea. On the second day of our voyage, we came to an island called Obbico, which is the largest of the Bahama Islands. We badly needed water, as we were exhausted after two days rowing under the hot sun.

We landed late in the evening and hauled the boat ashore to look for water and to sleep for the night. We searched the shore for water, but we found none. As darkness fell, we made a fire to scare away the wild animals,. We took it in turns to watch through the night, as the place we landed was surrounded by thick forest. We had very little rest that night, which we spent waiting for the morning.

As soon as dawn broke, we set off again in our boat, in the hope of finding help that day. We were now badly weakened by rowing the boat, as our sail was of no use. We were struggling greatly with the lack of freshwater to drink. We had nothing left to eat but salted beef, which we could not eat without water.

We toiled all day at the oars, within sight of the island, which was very long. That evening, we went ashore again and tied up our boat. We once again went to look for freshwater, feeling faint with the lack of it. We dug the earth and searched about all eventing, but we could not find a single drop. Terror arose amongst us, and we began to fear that only death would relieve us. Without freshwater, we could not touch our beef, which was as salty as the sea. We were also in terror of wild animals. When the unwelcome night fell, we again stood fearful watches. The next morning, we set off once more, in the faint hope of seeing a ship. We rowed as best we could, passing a number of small islands, but we saw no ships.

Around four o'clock, we went ashore on a small island in the desperate hope of finding water. We found leaves with a few drops of water on them, which we eagerly lapped. We then dug for water in several places, but with no luck. As we were digging, we found some very thick and black watery stuff, but none of us could touch it, except the Dutch creole man. He drank two pints of it, as if it were wine. We tried to catch fish, but could not. We began to give in to despair when the captain suddenly cried out, "A sail! A sail! A sail!"

This felt like being released from jail, and we all turned to look. Some of us began to fear that it was not a sail. Yet we launched the boat and steered towards it and, in half an hour, to our joy, we plainly saw that it was a ship. Our spirits revived, and we made towards her with all speed. As we came near, we saw that she was a little sloop, strangely full of people. Our captain, who was a Welshman, swore that they were pirates, and would kill us. I said that we must get aboard her even if we were to die for in the attempt, and that if they did not welcome us, we must fight them as best we could, as otherwise we would surely die.

This advice was taken and I believe the captain, myself, and the Dutchman, would have faced twenty men. We had two cutlasses and a musket and so we rowed alongside and immediately boarded her. There were about forty people on board. We were surprised to find that most of these were in the same situation as ourselves.

Most aboard were the crew of whaling schooner, which was wrecked two days before us about nine miles to the north. Some of the crew had taken to their boats to seek help, just as we had done. They too had left both people and property on a small island, and went looking for a ship. Like us, they were also headed to New Providence when they met this little sloop.

This little sloop was known as a wrecker. Its crew made a living from the many wrecks in these waters. They were going to take the crew of the whaling schooner to safety, but at the price of taking all the things belonging to the whaler. We told the people of wrecker's captain the state of our vessel, and we made the same deal with them.

We begged of them to go to our little island directly, as our people badly needed water. They agreed to go there first and two days later we arrived at the island, to the joy of those we had left behind. They had become badly in need of water in our absence. The wrecker couldn't carry or feed everyone on the journey to New Providence. So we left some of its crew to work on our wreck. We also left them our boat and sailed for New Providence.

We were fortunate to meet this wrecker, as New Providence was so far that we could never have made it in our little boat. The island of Abbico was much longer than we thought, and it took three or four days to sail the length of it to New Providence. When we arrived there we watered, and feasted on lobsters and other shellfish. This was a great relief, as our provisions and water were almost gone by the time we arrived.

We then continued our voyage; but the day after we left the island, a violent gale arose late in the evening. We were still in the shallow waters of the Bahama islands, and so we anchored to ride out the storm. Yet the winds became so severe that , we had to cut away our mast. The ship broke away from her anchors, and went aground several times in the shallow waters. Every moment, we expected the ship to go to pieces. We though each moment would be our last. The Welsh captain and my old sickly mate even fainted, as did many others, as death stared us in the face on every side.

Even the worst men on board began to call on God to help us and, sure enough, he did soon miraculously help us. At the height of the storm, the wind lulled for a few minutes and, although the swell was high beyond expression, two men who were strong swimmers, rowed to get the buoy at the end of our anchor, which we still could still see in the distance.

They rowed in a little punt belonging to the wrecker, which could only carry two men. They almost sank three times in their attempt to merely leave our ship, but they said they might as well die that way as any other. They had a coil of rope, and a little buoy, in their boat. These two intrepid heroes then paddled bravely away towards the anchor buoy. All eyes were fixed on them all the time, expecting every minute to be their last. The prayers of all those who remained in their senses were offered up to God.

These prayers were answered when the two men at last reached the buoy. Having tied the punt to it, they tied one end of their rope to the small buoy, which they had with them, and let it drift towards the ship. We threw out boat-hooks and ropes to catch the buoy as it drifted towards us. At last, we caught it and tied it to a large rope. They then pulled the large rope towards them and tied that to the anchor buoy. Once this was done, we all pulled for our lives, and dragged the ship safely into deep water, to the delight of all on board.

Two days later, the wind dropped, and the sea became smooth. We sent the punt ashore. We found our mast on the beach, and cut down some trees to mend it. As soon as the mast was in place, we set out again for New Providence.

Three days later, we finally arrived. When the people heard what we had suffered, they were very kind to us. They welcomed us warmly and showed great friendship. Soon after, all the free men amongst us went their separate ways. One merchant, who had a large sloop, told four of us that his ship was going to Georgia. He said we could work our passage there.

This seemed to be out our only way out. We helped to load the ship, though we were only paid by being given our food. When the ship was loaded, the captain told us she was going to Jamaica first. Heating this, I refused to go, fearing being taken into slavery once again. The others didn't have any money, so they had to accept this offer, although they did not like it.

I stayed in New Providence for about seventeen or eighteen days. During this time, I met many friends, who invited me to stay with them. I thought about staying on the island, as I liked the place a great deal. There were some free black people there who were very happy, and we passed the time pleasantly together, playing music under the lime and lemon trees. Yet I could not stay, as my heart was now set on England,

In the end, Captain Phillips hired a sloop to take the slaves he couldn't sell to Georgia. I agreed to go with him. When the ship was ready, I said farewell to New Providence, with some sadness.

At about four o'clock in the morning, we sailed for Georgia with a fair wind. At about eleven o'clock that morning a vicious squall sprung up and blew away most of our sails. As we were still amongst the islands, in a just a few minutes, the sloop ran onto the rocks. Luckily for us, the waves were not so angry. Through the hard work of our many crew, we managed to get the sloop off the rocks. The next day, we returned to Providence, where we refitted the sloop. Some of the people there swore that we must have had a spell put on us by somebody in Montserrat to have such bad luck. Others said that some of our slaves must be witches or wizards and that we would never arrive safely in Georgia. These things did not deter me. I said, "Let us again face the winds and seas, and swear not, but trust to God, and he will deliver us." We then set sail once more and, with hard work, in seven days' time we arrived safely in Georgia.

After we arrived, we went up to the town of Savannah. That evening , I went to stay in the house of a friend of mine, a black man named Mosa. We were very happy to see each other. After supper, we had a light till almost ten o'clock at night. About that time the watchmen came by on patrol. Seeing a light in the house, they knocked at the door. We invited them in to drink some punch with us. They asked me for some limes, which I happily gave them.

They then said I had to go to the watch house with them. I was very surprised at this, after our kindness to them. I asked them, "Why so?" They said that all black people who had a light in their house after nine o'clock were to be taken into custody, and had to pay a fine or be flogged. Some of the watchmen knew that I was a free man. Yet because my friend Mosa was a slave, and had his master to protect him, they did not treat him as they did me. I told them that I was a free man, who had just arrived from New Providence. I said that we're not making any noise, and that I was not a stranger in that place, but was very well known there.

I said, "what will you do with me?" They replied, "you shall see. But you must go to the watch house with us."

Now, whether they planned to take money from me, I didn't to know. I thought immediately of the time the oranges and limes were stolen from me at Santa Cruz. Yet seeing that nothing would persuade them to leave me be, I went with them to the watch house, where I stayed the night. Early the next morning, these ruffians flogged a black man and woman that they had in the watch house. They then told me that I would be flogged too.

I asked why, and if there was no law for free men? I told them if there was, I would have it put in force against them. But this only angered them even more and they instantly swore they would beat me as Doctor Perkins had. Just then, one of them, who was more humane than the rest, said that as I was a free man they could not by law justify holding me. I then sent for Doctor Brady, who was an honest and good man. As soon as he arrived to help me, they let me go.

This was not the only unhappy incident to occur with while I was in Savannah. One day, when I was just outside the town of Savannah, I was attacked by two white men, who tried to kidnap me. As soon as they attacked me, one of them said to the other, "This is the fellow we are looking for that you lost" and the other swore that I was a runaway slave. They came up to me and were about to grab me when I told them to keep off and that I had seen these tricks played on other free blacks, and they must not treat me so.

At this, they paused, and one said that I spoke English too well. I replied that I believed I did and that my mind was good too. I also mentioned that I had with me a stick equal to the occasion. Happily, however, it was not used. After we had talked a little, these rogues left me.

I stayed in Savannah some time, trying to get to Montserrat once more to see Mr. King, my old master, and then to bid a final farewell to the American part of the globe. In the end, I met with Captain John Bunton who had a sloop from Grenada, called the Speedwell. They were bound to the French island of Martinique, with a cargo of rice. I soon agreed to go aboard her.

Before I left Georgia, I met a black woman, whose child had died. She wanted a church burial service. Yet she could not get any white person to perform it. She asked me to do it. I told her I was no parson and also that the service done for the dead did not affect the soul. This did not satisfy her, and she begged me very hard. In the end, I agreed to act as a parson for the first time in my life.

As she was a respected woman, many white and black people came to the grave. I then took on my new role, and performed the funeral ceremony well. Then I bade adieu to Georgia and sailed for Martinique.

CHAPTER 9

TO ENGLAND AND THE ARCTIC

I left Georgia, disgusted with the place, and how I had been mistreated there. As we sailed for Martinique, I promised to never set foot in Georgia again.

My new captain navigated the ship better than the last one. After a pleasant voyage, we arrived in Martinique. I explored the island and found it very pleasant. I admired the town of St. Pierre. It is the main town of the island and built more in the European style than any other town in the West Indies. The slaves were also generally better treated here. They had more holidays, and looked better than those on the English islands.

After we had done our business, I asked to leave the ship, to get to Montserrat to bid farewell to Mr. King, and my other friends, before sailing for England in the July fleet. It was now May, and time was wasting. However, I had created a problem for myself. I had lent my captain some money. I told him that I needed it back to pay my way to England. The captain replied evasively. I soon began to fear losing my money.

I knew that I could not recover it in court. As in all the West Indies, a black man's testimony is not allowed against a white person. This meant I had to stay with the captain, until he would return my money. As we sailed from Martinique for the Grenades, I often asked the captain for my money but it was no use. To make matters worse, when we arrived in the Grenadines, the captain and the ship's owners quarrelled.

We were only allowed the food we had on board and I could not get my money or my wages. I could then have gotten my passage free to Montserrat had I been able to accept it. The worst thing of all was that it was now July, and all the ships in the islands would sail to England by the 26th of that month.

At last, after many requests, I got my money from the captain. I took the first vessel I could to St. Eustatia. From there I took in another ship to St. Kitts, where I arrived on the 19th of July. On the 22nd, I found a ship bound for Montserrat, I wanted to go aboard, but the captain would not take me on board until I should advertise my going off the island, as they feared I was an escaped slave. Every black freeman must advertise when he leaves an island, which I thought an unfair thing to make any free man do.

I told them I was in a hurry to get to Montserrat, and that I didn't have time to advertise, as it was late in the evening and the ship was about to sail. Yet the captain insisted and said he said he would not take me otherwise.

I knew that if I could not get to England that year, unless I left then. With a heavy heart, I went to try to advertise my departure, and to see who I could find to help me. Luckily I found some gentlemen I knew from Montserrat. I told them my situation, and asked for their help. Some of them went with me to the captain and told him they knew me to be a free man. The captain was then happy to take me aboard, to my great joy,

We set sail and I arrived at Montserrat the next day, after six months away. In that time I had escaped death more than once. I met my friends with a gladness of heart that was increased by my absence, and the dangers I had escaped. I was received with great friendship by all, but particularly by Mr. King. I told him of the fate of his sloop, the Nancy, and how she was wrecked.

I now learned with sorrow that Mr King's house had been washed away in my absence. A lake had burst at the top of a mountain which swept much of the town away. Mr. King had lost a great deal of property in the flood, and nearly lost his life.

I told him I intended to go to London, and that I had come to say farewell before I left. The good man said how fond he was of me, and that he was sad to see me think of leaving. He said I should stay there, as I was respected by the gentlemen of the island and that would do very well. He said that in a short time I might have land and slaves of my own. I thanked him for this friendly advice. I told him I wanted above all else to be in London. I asked him to forgive me, but I would have to go. I then asked if would be kind enough to give me a reference as to my good behaviour while in his service. He then kindly wrote these words:

Montserrat, January 26, 1767.

To all whom this may concern.

The bearer hereof, Gustavus Vassa, was my slave for upwards of three years, during which he has always behaved himself well, and discharged his duty with honesty and assiduity.

Robert King

I then left my kind master and prepared to leave for London. I immediately agreed with Captain John Hamer to be paid seven guineas to work my passage to London, on board a ship called the Andromache. On the 24th and 25th July, I had what are called "free dances" with many of my countrymen before I set off.

I sadly bade farewell to all my friends, and on the 26th of July 1767, I sailed for London. I was happy to find myself on one more board a ship. I was happier still to be on one steering the course I had long wished for.

With a light heart, I said farewell to Montserrat. Yet I also said farewell to the sound of the cruel whip and all the other dreadful instruments of torture. Farewell also, to the offensive sight of the violated chastity of the black females, which too often assaulted my eyes. Farewell also to oppression – even though this were for me less severe than for most of my countrymen. I said a last farewell to the angry, howling, dashing surf. I praised God for his mercy.

We had a fine voyage, and seven weeks later, we arrived at Cherry-Garden stairs in London. My longing eyes were once more treated to the sights of London, after having been gone over four years.

I received my wages. I had never earned seven guineas so quickly in my life. I now left the ship with thirty-seven guineas to my name. I was full of hope as I stepped ashore. I went first to see the Miss Guerins. I eventually found them at May's Hill, Greenwich. They were delighted to see me, and I was overjoyed to meet them. They were amazed at my story. They freely said that their cousin, Captain Pascal, had done me wrong.

I met Captain Pascal in Greenwich park a few days later. When he saw me, he was very surprised. He asked me how I had come back. I answered, "In a ship." He replied dryly, "I suppose you did not walk back to London on the water." I saw from his manner that he was not sorry for what he had done to me, and that I couldn't expect any kindness from him. I told him that he had treated me very badly, even though I had been a faithful servant to him for so many years. At this, he said nothing, but turned and walked away.

A few days later, I met Captain Pascal again at Miss Guerin's house, and asked him for my prize-money. He said there was none due to me and that if my prize money had been £10,000 he had the right to keep it all. I said that I had been told otherwise. He jokingly told me to take a lawsuit against him for the money. He said, "There are lawyers enough that will take the case, and you had better try it." I told him then that I would try it, which filled him with rage. Yet out of kindness to the ladies, I stayed still and said nothing more about my prize money.

Sometime later, the kind Guerin ladies asked me what I planned to do with myself, and how they could help me. I thanked them, and asked if I could please work as their servant. If not, I said that since I thirty-seven guineas I would be thankful if they could arrange for me to learn a trade so I could earn a living.

They politely said that they were sorry but it did not suit them to take me on as their servant. They then asked me what business I would like to learn. I said that I would like to learn hairdressing. They promised to help with this. Soon after, they introduced me to a Captain O'Hara, who treated me kindly, and found me a master hairdresser in Haymarket.

I worked with this man from September 1767 until February the following year. At that time, a neighbour also taught me to play the French horn. He used to play it so well that I became charmed by the instrument. I arranged for him to teach me, and I soon learned the joy of it. I loved playing this instrument, as my evenings alone were long, and I didn't like to be idle. Playing music soon filled up these empty hours.

At this time, I also met Rev. Gregory, who lived in the same court and ran an academy. I arranged for him to teach me more maths in his evening school. This he did as far as the rule of three and averaging. I was busy all the time I was there.

In February 1768, I got a job with Dr. Charles Irving in Pall Mall. He was well known for his experiments which discovered ways to make seawater fresh. I got plenty of practice hair-dressing there. Dr. Irving was an excellent master. He was kind and good natured and allowed to attend school in the evenings, which I thought a blessing. I thanked God and him for this.

My hard work for Dr Irving saw me become favoured by three of my teachers. Each put a great deal of effort into teaching me and all were very kind to me. Yet my wages were two thirds lower than I had earned before, for I only earned £12 a year. I soon found that this was not enough to pay my teachers and my own expenses.

My thirty-seven guineas had by then worn away to just one. I thought it best to go to sea again, to make more money. I had been a sailor since childhood, and was good at it. I had also a great desire to see Turkey. In May 1768, I told the doctor that I wanted to go to sea again and we parted on friendly terms.

The same day, I went into the city in quest of a master. I was lucky with who I asked; for I soon heard of a gentleman who had a ship going to Italy and Turkey, and he wanted a man who could dress hair well. I was overjoyed at this, and went immediately on board his ship. The ship was fitted up with great taste, and I looked forward to sailing in her.

As I didn't find the gentleman on board, I was directed to his lodgings, where I met him the next day. I have him a demonstration of my hairdressing. He liked it so much that he hired me immediately. I was delighted, as the ship, its master, and the voyage, were all to my liking.

The ship was called the Delaware, and my master's name was John Jolly. He was a smart and good humoured man, who I was happy to serve. We sailed from England in July 1768, and our voyage was extremely pleasant. We went to Nice, Villa Franca and Leghorn, known to the Italians as Livorno. I was charmed by the richness and beauty of each place and was struck by the many elegant buildings.

We had always had plenty of good wines and rich fruits, which I was very fond of. I often could explore these places, for my captain always lodged on shore. I also learned navigation from the mate, which delighted me.

When we left Italy, we had delightful sailing among the Greek islands, and from there we sailed to Smyrna in the Greek part of Turkey. This is a very ancient city. Its houses are built of stone. Most have graves right next to them, which sometimes makes them look like churchyards. Food and drink are very plentiful in this city, and good wine costs less than a penny a pint. The grapes, pomegranates, and many other fruits were also the richest and largest I had ever tasted.

The people are good looking and strong. They always treated me with great respect and civility. I believe they are fond of black people. Several invited me to stay with them, although they keep the franks, or Christians, separate, and do not allow them to live amongst them.

I was amazed to see no women in the shops, and rarely in the streets. Whenever I saw them, they were covered with a veil from head to foot, so that I could not see their faces, except when they uncovered their faces to look at me, which they sometimes did out of curiosity.

I was surprised to see how the Greeks are kept down by the Turks. This was in some ways like the way black people are in the West Indies are kept down by the white people. The less refined Greeks also dance much as we do in my nation.

On the whole, during our five-month stay in Smyrna, I found I that liked both the place and the Turks a great deal. I could not help noticing one remarkable thing there. The tails of the sheep are flat, and so large, that the tail of a lamb can weigh up to thirteen pounds. Their fat is white and rich, and excellent in puddings, in which it is often used. Our ship was soon richly loaded with silks, and other luxurious things, and so we sailed back to England.

In May 1769, soon after we returned from Turkey, our ship made another delightful voyage to Oporto in Portugal. We arrived at the time of the carnival. When we arrived, we were told that there were 36 laws we had to carefully observe, with very heavy penalties if we broke any of them. Anyone who was found with a Protestant bible would be imprisoned and flogged and sent into slavery for ten years. None of us dared to go ashore until the Inquisition had come on board and searched for anything illegal, especially bibles. The bibles we had were sent ashore to be held by the authorities until the ships were leaving.

I saw many magnificent sights in Oporto. In the garden of Eden, many of the clergy and laity went in procession with the host, singing Te Deum. I was curious to go into some of their churches, but could not go in without sprinkling holy water upon myself at the entrance. Out of curiosity, and a wish to be holy, I sprinkled hold water on myself, but I found myself none the better for it. Oporto is a well built and pretty town with fine views, and abundant provisions. Our ship took on board a load of wine, and we sailed for London, arriving there in July.

Our next voyage was to the Mediterranean. The ship was again got ready, and in September we sailed for Genoa in Italy. This was one of the finest cities I had ever seen, with noble marble buildings, and many fascinating fountains.

The churches were magnificent, and richly adorned inside and out. Yet all this grandeur was to my eyes disgraced by the galley slaves, who were kept in pitiful and wretched conditions, both there and in other parts of Italy.

We spent some weeks in Genoa, buying many different things. We then sailed to Naples, which is a charming and very clean city. The Bay of Naples is the most beautiful I have ever seen. The city's ship harbours are excellent. It was extraordinary to see grand operas here on Sunday nights, which were even attended by royalty. I, like these great ones, saw those wonderful sights.

While in Naples, I had a perfect view of the eruption of Mount Vesuvius. We were so near that the ashes from it used to land thick on our deck. After we had finished our business in Naples, we sailed with a fair wind again to Smyrna, where we arrived in December. A seraskier, or officer, took a liking to me there, and asked me to stay. He even offered me two wives, but I refused the temptation. The merchants there travel in caravans or large companies. I have seen many caravans from India, some with hundreds of camels, all laden with different goods. The people who travel with these caravans are quite brown.

Among other things, they brought with them a great quantity of locust fruit, which are sweet and pleasant to taste. Each kind of goods is sold in a particular street. I always found the Turks to be very honest in their dealings. However, they let no Christians into their mosques. I was sad at this, as I enjoyed seeing the different ways people worshipped wherever I went.

A plague broke out while we were in Smyrna, and we stopped taking goods into the ship until it was over. Out ship was by then richly laden and so, in March 1770, we sailed for England. One day an accident happened and the ship nearly went up in flames. A black cook who was melting some fat, put the pan into the fire under the deck, which immediately began to blaze up very high. In his fright, the poor cook became almost white. Luckily, we got the fire out without it doing too much harm. After a long passage, we arrived in Standgate creek in July. At the end of 1770, my noble captain, the ship, and I all separated.

In April 1771, I shipped myself as a steward with Captain William Robertson of the ship Grenada Planter. I dared to once more try my fortune in the West Indies. We sailed from London for Madeira and then to Barbados and the Grenadines.

When we were in the Grenadines, I had some goods to sell and I met again some of my former West India customers. A white man from the islands bought some goods from me which were worth quite a few pounds. He made many fine promises to pay me as usual, but without any intention doing so. He had also bought goods from others from our ship without paying. When our ship was loaded and about to sail, I asked him for my money and he threatened me and another black man he had bought goods from. We found that we were more likely to get blows than payment.

We complained to the justice of the peace, Mr. MacIntosh. We told him of the man's tricks, and begged him to find justice for us. Yet because we were black men, although we were free, we could not get any remedy. Luckily for us, this man had also tricked three white sailors, who could not get a farthing from him. They happily joined us, and we all went in search of him. When we found him, I took him out of a house and threatened him with vengeance.

When he saw he was likely to be handled roughly, the rogue offered us some small payment, but nothing near what we were due. This angered us even more; and some said we should cut his ears off, but he begged hard for mercy. This was given to him, after we had stripped him. He thanked us for letting him go, as he was glad to get off so easily. He then ran into the bushes, wishing us a good voyage. We went aboard, and soon set sail for England.

Just as our ship got under way, I went down into the cabin to do some work, with a lighted candle in my hand. In my hurry, I put it into barrel of gunpowder, forgetting what was in it. The candle was about to set the gunpowder, when I saw it and snatched it out – just in time. I was so overcome with terror that I fainted.

After twenty-eight days at sea, we arrived in England, and I left the ship. I was a roving soul, and wanted to see as many different parts of the world as I could. Later that year, I became a steward to Captain David Watt of a fine large ship called the Jamaica. In December 1771, we sailed for Nevis and Jamaica. I found Jamaica to be a large and well-populated island. There was a vast number of black people there, who were abused and punished by the white people, just as elsewhere in the West Indies.

In Jamaica, there are black people whose job it is to flog slaves. They go about the island for their dark work, and their usual pay is from one to four bits. I saw many cases of cruel punishment of slaves in the short time I was in Jamaica. I saw one poor fellow tied up and kept hanging by the wrists above from the ground. Then, some heavy weights were fixed to his ankles. Strung up in this cruel way, he was then flogged unmercifully.

I heard that there were two masters well known for cruelty on the island. They had staked up two black people naked, and in two hours they were stung to death by insects. I heard a gentleman I knew tell my captain that he sentenced a black man to be burnt alive for attempting to poison his overseer.

Before I had been long on the island, a Mr. Smith of Port Morant bought goods from me worth twenty-five pounds sterling. When I asked him for payment, he said he would beat me, and threatened to put me in jail. One time, he would say I was going to set his house on fire, another he would swear I was going to run away with his slaves. I was astonished at such lies from a person who was considered a gentleman. I had no access to the law, so I had no choice but to allow him to get away with this.

In Kingston, I was surprised to see that many Africans gathered together on Sundays. The largest gathering was at a place called Spring Path. Here the different nations of Africa met and danced in style of their own country. They still kept to most of their native customs. For example, when they bury their dead, they put food, pipes, tobacco and other things in the grave with the body, just as in Africa.

When our ship was loaded, we sailed for London. We arrived in London in August and I called on my old employer, Dr. Irving. He offered me a job again. I was by now tired of the sea, and I gladly took it. I was very happy to be living with this gentleman once more. We were kept busy reducing old Neptune's domain, by purifying seawater and making it fresh.

I worked with Dr Irving until May 1773, but my daily life was to again be changed by the promise of fame and adventure. Dr Irving had heard of an expedition that was getting fitted out to find out a new passage to India by the North Pole. This was to be led by the Honourable John Constantine Phipps, who later became Lord Mulgrave. Our ship for this voyage of exploration was his Majesty's sloop of war, Race Horse.

Dr Irving was keen on this adventure and so we began to prepare for the voyage. I joined him on board the Race Horse on the 24th day of May 1773. We sailed to Sheerness, where we were joined by his Majesty's sloop Carcass, commanded by Captain Lutwidge. On the 4th of June we sailed towards the North Pole. By the 15th of June we were off Shetland.

On this day, the ship was nearly blown up. It was so filled with provisions, that there was very little room on board for anyone. I had decided to keep a journal of this interesting voyage, which I wrote in the little cabin where I slept, which was the doctor's store room. This little place was stuffed with all manner of things that could easily burn, including tar and aquafortis, which can be explosive. That evening, as I was writing my journal, I took the candle out of the lantern. A single spark touched the tar, it immediately went ablaze.

I saw nothing but death before me, and expected to be the first to perish in the flames. The alarm was spread, and many ran to help put out the fire. All this time, I was in the flames - my shirt and the handkerchief on my neck, were burnt, and I was almost smothered by the smoke.

Just as I was giving up hope, some people brought blankets and threw them on the flames, and the fire was put out. I was severely reprimanded by the officers, and strictly ordered never to go in there again with a light. My own fears helped me obey this order for a time but, in the end, as I couldn't write my journal in any other part of the ship, I again stole fearfully into the same cabin with a light. On the 20th of June, we began to use Dr. Irving's apparatus for making salt water fresh. I used to look after the distillery. I often purified forty gallons of water a day. The water I distilled was perfectly pure, and tasted good. It was free from salt and was often used on the ship. On the 28th of June, we were above the Arctic Circle, in latitude 78 degrees north. We made it to Greenland, where I was surprised to find that the sun did not set.

The weather was extremely cold and as we sailed northeast, we saw many very high and strange icebergs; and many very large whales. The whales used to come close to our ship, and blow the water high up into the air. One morning, there were vast quantities of sea-horses around the ship, which neighed exactly like any other horses. We fired some harpoon guns at them, in order to take some, but we could not get any.

On June the 30th, the captain of a Greenland ship came on board, and told us that three ships were lost in the ice. Yet we still held our course until July the 11th, when we were stopped by one impassable body of ice. We ran along it from east to west above ten degrees. On the 27th of July, we were above 80 degrees north. On the 29th and 30th of July we saw an enormous plain of smooth unbroken ice stretching to the horizon. We tied the ship on to a piece of ice that was eight yards thick.

We generally had sunshine, and constant daylight; which gave the whole unusual, striking scene a cheerful look.

The reflection of the sun from the ice also gave the clouds a most beautiful appearance.

We killed many different animals at this time, including nine polar bears. Though they had nothing in their bellies but water, they were all very fat. We used to lure them to the ship by burning feathers or skins, before killing them. I thought them rough to eat, but some of the ship's crew relished them.

Once, the crew in the small boat fired at and wounded a sea-horse, which dived to escape. Soon after, it came up with it a number of others. They all joined in an attack upon the boat, and they nearly capsized it. A boat from the Carcass came to help ours, and they went away, after taking an oar from one of the men. Happily, no harm was done. Though we wounded several of these animals, we never captured one.

We remained here until the 1st of August when the two ships got completely stuck in the ice, after loose ice drifted in from the sea, surrounded us, and then froze. This made our situation dreadfully worrying. By the 7th of August, we were worried that the ships would be squeezed to pieces. The officers held a meeting to decide how best to save our lives. They decided that we should try to escape by dragging our boats along the ice towards the sea - which was farther off than any of us thought. This decision filled us with despair, for we had very little chance of escaping alive that way.

We sawed away some of the ice around the ships to keep it from damaging them and so we kept them in a kind of pond. We then began to drag the boats as best as we could towards the sea. After two or three days labour, we had made very little progress. Hope began to fail us, and I began to give up myself for lost.

While we were at this hard work, I once fell into a pond we had made amongst some loose ice, and was nearly drowned. Thankfully, some men were nearby helped me out. Our terrible situation meant we had a constant fear of dying in the ice. This caused me to think of eternity in way I never had before. The fear of death was hourly upon me. I shuddered at the thought of death, and doubted a happy eternity if I should die as I was.

We all knew we would not last long on the ice after leaving the ships, which were now out of sight, miles away. Pale fear seized every face. Men who had been blasphemers in their distress called upon the God of heaven for help. In this time of utter need, he heard us - against all hope. On the eleventh day of the ships being stuck in the ice, and the fourth day our towing the boats away, the wind suddenly direction. The weather suddenly became mild, and the ice broke towards the sea, which was to the southwest of us. Many of us got on board again and, with all our might, we sailed the ships into every bit of open water we could find, with all the sail we could carry.

This seemed to us like a reprieve from death, as now we had a chance to survive. We made signals for the boats and the rest of the people. Happy were the men who rushed aboard. We steered carefully through the pack ice, until we got into open water again, about thirty hours later.

As soon as we were out of danger ,we anchored and repaired the ships. On the 19th of August we sailed from this cold extremity of the world, where climate gives neither food nor shelter. Not a tree or shrub of any kind grows upon those barren rocks. It is but one empty waste of ice, which even the constant sun for six months of the year cannot melt.

The days shortened as we sailed to the southward. On the 28th of August in the latitude 73 degrees, it was dark by ten o'clock at night. On September the 10th, in latitude 58, we met a very severe gale of wind and high waves. We shipped a great deal of water in the space of ten hours. We had to work our pumps hard for a whole day. One wave struck the ship with more force than any I had seen before. It laid her under water for some time, and we thought she was had gone down. Three boats were washed from the deck, and every other moveable thing on the deck were also washed away including the many interesting things we had brought from Greenland. To lighten the ship, we had to toss some of our guns overboard. We saw another ship, in very great distress, with her masts gone, but we were unable to help her.

We lost sight of the Carcass till the 26th of September. Soon after we saw land at the east of England, she met with us. From there, we sailed for London and on the 30th of August, we came to Deptford after four months away. So ended our Arctic voyage, to the joy of all aboard. We had explored nearly to 81 degrees north, and 20 degrees east. This was much farther than any navigator had ever ventured before. We had proved that it was impossible to sail to India by the North Pole.

CHAPTER 10

DARK NIGHT OF THE SOUL

Once our voyage to the North Pole was over, I returned to London with Doctor Irving. I continued working for him for some time. I began to seriously think about the dangers I had escaped. My brushes with death on my last voyage made a lasting impression on my mind. This made me reflect deeply on the state of my soul, and to seek God with a full heart, before it was too late.

In time, I left my employer, Doctor Irving, and moved to Coventry Court, Haymarket. I was still deeply concerned about the salvation of my soul. This became my main focus. Yet I knew nobody who agreed with me on questions of religion, or who could help me to grow in faith. I didn't know where to turn. Firstly, I visited my neighbouring churches, two or three times a day for many weeks. Still, I was not satisfied. Something was missing which I could not find.

I found more heartfelt spirituality when reading my bible at home than when attending church. I tried other faiths. I went among the Quakers, where the word of God was neither read or preached. Yet I was as much in the dark as ever. I then looked into the Roman Catholic teachings but was not satisfied. In the end, I went to the Jews, which was no use, as the fear of eternity still harassed my mind. I did not know where to find shelter. In the end, I decided to read the four gospels and to join whatever faith I found following these teachings most closely.

I went on in this way, without anyone to guide me on the path to eternal life. I asked many people questions about how we went to heaven and was told different things. I was staggered. I could not find anyone more righteous or devoted than myself at this time. Nobody in my circle of friends kept the ten commandments fully. I was so righteous in my own eyes, that I was sure I was well ahead of the others, by keeping eight out of ten.

I also thought those who called themselves Christians were not so honest or good as the Turks. I began to think the Muslim faith was a safer way of salvation. In this way, I went on - caught between hope and fear.

The comforts I enjoyed were playing the French horn and dressing hair. So life went on for some months. In the end, I decided to set out for Turkey, to spend the rest of my life there. It was now early in the spring of 1774. I found captain John Hughes, commander of a ship called Anglicania, which was fitting out on the river Thames, bound for Smyrna in Turkey.

I went on board with him as a steward. I also recommended to him a very clever black man as a cook, named John Annis. This man had once lived for years on the island of St Kitts with Mr. William Kirkpatrick. He left his former master by agreement, but Mr Kirkpatrick tried many tricks to get the poor man back. He had asked many captains who traded to St. Kitts to kidnap him. Mr. Kirkpatrick heard that John was on board our ship. He came to our ship at Union Stairs on Easter Monday with two wherry boats and six men. They forcibly took him off from the ship, with the crew and the chief mate watching. I believe that this was a conspiracy. It was a disgrace for the captain and mate to allow this. Nor was he paid a penny of his wages, which were about five pounds. I proved to be the only friend he had. I tried hard to get him back his liberty, having known the lack of freedom myself.

I found out the name of the ship he was held in, but she had sailed the first tide after he was taken on board. I then tried to arrest Mr. Kirkpatrick, who was about setting off for Scotland. I got a writ of *habeas corpus* for him, and got a bailiff to go with me to St. Paul's, where he lived but he had kept a look out.

Because I was known to him, I used a trick. I whitened my face so that they would not recognise me. He did not leave his house that night, and he had a gentleman in his house pretending to be him, to avoid arrest. The next morning, I came up with a plan. I told to the bailiff, to bring him to a judge, as the writ directed. The bailiff got into the house, and hauled him to court. When he got to court, he said that he was not the right man, and he was released on bail.

I went to the philanthropist, Granville Sharp, who welcomed me with kindness and gave me all the advice I needed. I left in the hope that would get John his freedom. Yet this lawyer proved untrue. He took my money, and did not do any good for the case. When poor John arrived at St. Kitts, he was staked to the ground with four pins through a rope, two on his wrists, and two on his ankles. He was cut and flogged unmercifully, and had irons cruelly put around his neck. I had two very moving letters from him, while he was there. He remained a slave, until kind death released him from the hands of his tyrants.

During this bad business, I thought the state of my soul worse than any man's. My mind was disturbed and I often wished for death. Yet I knew I was not ready for that awful summons. I had suffered the evils of men, and was worried about the state of my soul. These things brought me low. I became a burden to myself, and saw everything around me as emptiness and vanity. Nothing could not salve my troubled mind.

I wished to see Turkey again. At that time, I wished to go and never again return to England. I soon went on board a ship bound for Turkey, Wester Hall, as a steward. Yet I was stopped from going by my old captain, Mr. Hughes, and others. Everything seemed against me, and the only comfort I found were the holy scriptures.

I felt that there is nothing new under the sun and that I had to I submit to my fate. I went on heavily through life, often murmuring against the fate God had given me. I even began to swear, and wished to be anything but a human being. In these torments, God answered me with awful visions that came in the night, when a deep sleep falls upon men. He let me began to understand the awful scene of judgment day, and that no unclean person, and no unholy thing, can enter the kingdom of God.

I then would have changed my place with the lowest worm of the earth. I was ready to tell the mountains and rocks to fall on me. I then asked my Creator to give me a small space of time to repent my sins. God granted my request, and my sense of his mercy became so great that when I awoke, my strength failed me. I got out of bed and dressed, and begged God to never again let me fail.

God is full of compassion to poor rebels such as us. He heard me, and answered. I clearly saw the bad use I had made of the gifts I had been given. They were given to me to glorify God. I thought I had better use them well, and so enter into eternal life, instead of abusing them and being cast into hell fire. I prayed for God to send me holy people to help me. I appealed to the searcher of hearts, but I was in darkness. I soon hated the house I stayed in, because God's holy name was taken vainly in it.

I had a great desire to read the bible all day at home. But as I had no quiet place to read in the house, I left the house in the daytime, rather than stay amongst the wicked people there. As I was out walking one day, God directed me to a house where there was an old seafaring man, who had felt the love of God deeply in his heart. He began to talk with me. I had never before heard the love of Christ spoken of in such a clear way.

I had more questions than time. A dissenting minister soon joined our conversation. He asked me where I went to church, if I did. I said that I attended St. James's, St. Martin's, and St. Ann's in Soho too.

He replied, "So, are a churchman." I answered that I was. He then invited me to a love feast at his chapel that evening. I accepted the offer, and thanked him. After he went away, I spoke again with the old Christian, which made me deeply happy.

My conversation with these two men, lifted my heavy spirit more than anything had in many months. The hours seemed long before I went to this supposed banquet, as I wished so for the company of these kind men. Their company pleased me deeply. I thought it very kind to ask me, a stranger, to a feast. Yet how strange it was to have a feast in a chapel!

I arrived at the chapel and the old man was there. He kindly seated me. I was astonished to see the place filled with people. There were many ministers there, but there were no signs of eating and drinking.

They began to sing hymns and to pray. I didn't know what to make of this, as I'd never seen the like before. Some guests began to speak of their experiences, and much was said of the unspeakable mercy of God. This I knew well, and I could heartily join them. But when they spoke of life after death, they seemed certain of their closeness God. They were sure that no one could separate them from the love of Christ, or take them from his hands. This filled me with both confusion and admiration.

I did not know what to think of this group. My heart was drawn to them, and I wished to be as happy as them. I believed that they were different from the wicked world outside. Their language and singing were harmonious. I was overcome, and wished to live and die this way.

In the end, they produced baskets full of buns, which they shared. Each person there spoke with those near them, sharing food and water. I had never seen this kind of Christian fellowship before. Nor did I imagine I would on this earth. It reminded me of what I had read in the holy scriptures, of the early Christians, who loved each other and broke bread together. The group even went from house to house. This feast lasted about four hour ending in singing and prayer.

This was the first soul feast I ever went to. That single day had given me many things, spiritual and worldly, sleeping and waking, judgment and mercy. I could only admire the goodness of God, in sending the blind sinner on such a good path. He had shown mercy in answering the prayers of a prodigal son, who wanted to return home.

After this experience, I was resolved to win heaven if I could. I was sure that I would find it at the feet of Jesus. I saw that time was short, eternity long - and very near. I saw those ready for that midnight call as blessed. For the judge of all, living and dead, is coming.

The next day, I went to Holborn, to see my new friend, the old man. He and his wife were at work weaving silk weaving. His wife was kind, and they seemed happy together. They were glad to see me, and I them. I sat down, and we spoke about spiritual things.

Our conversation was delightful, educational and pleasant. As I reluctantly left, they lent me a little book, called "The Conversion of an Indian." It was written as questions and answers. The poor Indian man had come over the sea to London, to find out about the Christian's God. This book was of great use to me, and it strengthened my faith. They told me to call on them whenever I wished.

I prayed that the many evils I felt within might be taken away. I prayed that I might be weaned from my old friends, who were more carnal. This prayer was quickly heard and answered. I was soon amongst those which scripture calls the excellent of the earth. I heard the gospel, and my heart and deeds were laid open by the preachers. The way of salvation by Christ was made plain. So I went on happily for almost two months. I once heard of a man who had left this life in full confidence of heaven. I was astonished by this. and asked how he had this knowledge. I was told that if I did not experience a new birth, and the forgiveness of my sins through Christ before I died, I could not enter the kingdom of heaven.

I knew not what to think of this, and said I kept eight commandments out of ten. Then I was told that I did not, and could not, as no man ever kept the commandments. I thought this strange. It puzzled me much for weeks. I then asked my friend why the commandments of God were given, if we could not be saved by them? He replied, "The law is a schoolmaster to bring us to Christ," who alone could keep the commandments, and fulfilled them for his chosen people - those he had given living faith to. The sins of the chosen were already forgiven and if I did not experience the same before my death, God would say "Go ye cursed," for God was as true to the wicked, as he is in showing mercy to the chosen.

I was wounded at this, and I asked him if he was to die that moment, was he sure he'd enter the kingdom of God? I asked, 'Do you know that your sins are forgiven?" He answered that he did. Then confusion and anger seized me. I was staggered by this doctrine. I did not know what to believe. Were we saved by works, or by faith in Christ? I asked him to tell me how I might know if my sins were forgiven. He said none but God alone could do this. I told him this was very mysterious, but he said it was a matter of fact. He quoted scripture to prove his the point, to which I could not reply.

He told me to beg God to show me the true state of my soul. I thought the prayer very short and odd. I thought these things well over, wondered how a man could know his sins were forgiven. I wished God would reveal this to me. I then went to Westminster chapel, where I was told that men had no cause to complain being punished for their sins. God was just in his dealings. He showed justice in the eternal punishment of the wicked.

The seemed to me like a two-edged sword. It gave me both joy and fear about my soul. The preacher said he would examine all who wished to eat at the Lord's table. I thought of my good works, but doubted I was ready to receive the sacrament. I was full of thought until the day I was to be examined. I went to the chapel in distress that day.

I spoke with the reverend gentleman. The first thing he asked was, what I knew of Christ. I told him I believed in him, and had been baptised in his name. "Then," he said, "when were you brought to the knowledge of God? and how were you convinced of sin?"

I did not know what he meant by these questions. I told him I kept eight commandments out of ten, but that I sometimes swore on board ships, and sometimes when ashore, and that I sometimes broke the sabbath. He then asked me if I could read. I answered, "Yes." "

Then," said he, "do you not read in the bible, he that offends in one point is guilty of all?" I said, "Yes." Then he told me that one sin not forgiven was as able to damn a soul, as one leak could sink a ship.

I was struck with awe. The minister reminded me of the shortness of time, and the length of eternity. He did not allow me to take communion, but told me to read the scriptures, to hear the word preached, and to pray. I thanked him, and left determined to follow his advice.

During this time, I was out of work. As I couldn't find a suitable job in London, I had to go to sea again. I was hired as steward on a ship called the Hope, under Captain Richard Strange. We were bound from London to Cadiz in Spain.

Soon after going aboard, I heard the name of God blasphemed. I feared I might catch this horrible disease. I thought if I now sinned, after having life and death set clearly before me, I would certainly go to hell. My mind was distressed. I became unhappy with the commandments, as I could not be saved by what I had done. I hated all things, and wished I had never been born. Confusion seized me, and I wished to be annihilated.

One day, I was standing on the very edge of the stern of the ship, thinking to drown myself, when scripture came suddenly to mind: "no murderer has eternal life in him". Then, I paused, and thought myself the unhappiest man living. I knew God was kinder to me than I deserved. I was better off than many others. I then began to fear death again. I fretted, mourned, and prayed, until I became a burden to myself, and others.

In the end, I decided it would be better to beg for bread ashore, than to go to sea with those who did not fear God. I asked the captain to let me go three times, but he would not. Each time, he encouraged me to stay with him. All on board showed me great kindness. Yet I was unwilling to go to sea again. Some of my religious friends said going to sea was my lawful calling, and that it was my duty to obey.

Mr. G.S. the governor of Tothil-fields Bridewell, especially pitied me, advised me, and prayed for me. Soon, my burden was removed, and I found a heartfelt submission to God's will. The good man gave me a pocket Bible and the next day I went on board again. We sailed for Spain, and I found favour with the captain.

We sailed from London on the 4th of September. We had a delightful voyage to Cadiz, where we arrived the 23rd of September. Cadiz is a strong, rich city, with fine commanding views. Spanish galleons visit its port, and some arrived while we were there. I had time to read the scriptures. I wrestled hard in fervent prayer with God, who said he would hear the groanings and sighs of the poor in spirit. I found this proven, to my astonishment.

On the morning of the 6th of October, I thought I would either see or hear something supernatural that day. I had a secret intuition that something would happen. It pleased God to enable me to wrestle with him, as Jacob did. I prayed that if sudden death struck, I might be at Christ's feet.

That evening, I was reading the fourth chapter of the Acts, and reflecting on my past actions. I began to think I had lived a moral life, and that I had a proper ground to believe

I might have divine favour. Still not knowing whether salvation was to be had partly for our own good deeds, or only as the gift of God.

In this confusion, God's light shone in my soul. I clearly saw, with the eye of faith, the crucified Saviour bleeding on the cross on Mount Calvary. The scriptures became an unsealed book. I saw myself as a condemned criminal under the law. I saw the Jesus in his humiliation, bearing my guilt, sin, and shame. I then clearly understood that by the law alone, no man could be saved. I then understood what it was to be born again. The word of God was sweet to taste, sweeter than honey. Christ was revealed to my soul as divine. These heavenly moments were as life to the dead.

At that moment, everything that happened to me - from the day I was taken from my parents, to that hour - seemed if it had just happened. I was aware of the hand of God, which guided and protected me. God pursued me, even though I insulted and disregarded him. This mercy melted me down.

When I saw my low state, I wept, seeing what I owed to grace. Now, the African was willing to be saved by Jesus Christ. I would rely on nothing else. The amazing things of that hour can never be told. I felt an astonishing change. The weight of sin, the jaws of hell, and the fear of death, lost their horror. I thought death would be the best friend I ever had.

I was bathed in tears, and said, "What am I that God should look on me, the vilest of sinners?" I felt a deep concern for my mother and friends, which caused me to pray deeply. In the abyss of thought, I saw many people in an awful state, without God or hope.

When I left my cabin, I told some of the crew what God had done for me, but none could understand me. I seemed a barbarian to them, in talking of the love of Jesus. His name was to me a balm. It was sweet to my soul. But to them, it was a rock of offence.

Every hour until I returned to London, I longed to be with people I could tell of the wonders of God's love towards me. I had strange feelings within, that few know. The bible became my only companion and comfort. I prized it, and thanked God that I could read it for myself. The worth of a soul cannot be told. Whenever I looked in the bible, I saw new things, and its words gave me comfort.

Its promises spoke powerfully to me: "All things whatsoever ye shall ask in prayer, believing, ye shall receive," and "Peace I leave with you, my peace I give unto you."

I saw the Christ as the fountain of life, and the well of salvation. He had brought me by a path I did not know, and made crooked paths straight. So I was confirmed in the truths of the bible, on which every soul living must stand or fall eternally. May God give you understanding.

To those who believe, all things are possible. But to those that do not believe, nothing is pure.

During this time, we stayed at Cadiz until our ship was loaded. We sailed on the 4th of November and had a good passage to London. On my return I had but one text which puzzled me. One day I went to Blackfriars church, and, to my great surprise, Reverend Mr. Romaine preached from that very text. He very clearly showed the difference between human works and free will. I went to Westminster Chapel, and saw some of my old friends, who were glad when they saw the wonderful change that God had made in me. I was again examined at that the chapel, and was allowed to take communion, in fellowship with them. I rejoiced in spirit, with a song in my heart to God. Now my only wish was to dissolve, and to be with Christ -but sadly, I must wait for my appointed time.

CHAPTER 11

THE MUSKITO SHORE

When our ship was ready for sea, the captain asked me to go with him once more. I felt as happy as I could be in this life, so I refused at first. However, the advice of my friends won out, and I went aboard to sail again for Cadiz in March 1775.

We had a very good passage, without accident, until we arrived off the Bay of Cadiz. On Sunday, as we were going into the harbour, the ship struck a rock and lost a plank, just above to the keel. As the water gushed in, the crew were in great confusion, and began with to call upon God to have mercy on them. Although I could not swim, and saw death coming, I felt no fear, as I had no desire to live. I even rejoiced in spirit, thinking that death would be a glory. But my time had not yet come. The crew near to me were astonished to see me so calm, but I told them of the peace of God.

At the time, there were many large Spanish ships full of people crossing the channel. When they saw we were in danger, a number of them came alongside us. We began to work, with some men at our three pumps, while the rest unloaded the ship as fast as possible. As we had only struck a single rock called the Porpus, we soon floated off it, as the tide rose. We then ran the ship ashore at the nearest place possible, to keep her from sinking. After many tides, we had her repaired.

When we finished our business at Cadiz, we went to Gibraltar, and from there to Malaga, on the Spanish Mediterranean coast. This was a very pleasant and rich city, with one of the finest cathedrals I had ever seen. The cathedral had taken over fifty years to build, and it was not quite finished. Much of the inside was completed and it was highly decorated with the richest marble columns and many superb paintings. It was lighted occasionally by an amazing number of wax candles of different sizes, some of which were as thick as a man's thigh. These were only lit on feast days.

I was shocked at the custom of bull fighting which took place on Sunday evenings - to the scandal of Christianity. I told a priest I met why I disliked this. I often argued about religion with the reverend father, who tried to bring me into his church, as I tried to convert him to mine.

During these discussions, I used to produce my Bible, to show him where his church was in error. He then said he had been in England, and that it was very wrong that everyone there read the Bible. I told him that Christ wanted us to read the Scriptures. Hoping to convert me, he said I should go to one of the Spanish universities, where I could have a free education. He told me that if I was made a priest, I might even pope, as Pope Benedict had been a black man. As I loved to learn, I thought about this for a time. Yet it would be hypocrisy to embrace his offer, as I could not in conscience believe in the opinions of his church. We parted, without having changed each other's views.

Having taken on board fine wines, fruits, and coins, we proceeded to Cadiz, where we took aboard two tons more of coin. We then sailed for England in the month of June. At about latitude 42 degrees north, the wind went against us for several days, and the ship did not sail more than six or seven miles towards London in all those days. This made the captain very worried and cross I was very sorry to hear God's holy name blasphemed by him. One day, a young gentleman on board, who was a passenger, criticised the captain for this, saying we should be thankful to God for all things. He said that though the wind was against for us, it was fair for others, who perhaps needed it more than we did. I loudly agreed with this young gentleman. I expected that the captain would be very angry with me for this, but he said nothing.

That night I dreamed I saw a boat just off the starboard side. exactly at half past one o'clock. The following day, the 21st of June, the following day at noon as we had dined in the cabin, the man at the helm cried out, "A boat!" This brought my dream to mind. I jumped on deck saw a little boat some way off, just as in my dream.

We stopped our ship in the high seas, and the small boat came alongside. Its crew of eleven miserable men came aboard. Had we not stopped for them, they would have died within the hour. They were half-drowned, without food, a compass or water. They only had a bit of an oar to steer with, and they were at the mercy of the waves. As soon as they came aboard, they went on their knees, and lifted their hands and voices to heaven, thanking God. For he satisfies the longing soul, and fills the hungry with goodness.

The poor distressed captain of this small boat said "the Lord is good for, seeing that I am not ready to die, he gave me time to repent." I was very glad to hear this and I later spoke to him of God. These men were Portuguese, and had been in a brig loaded with corn, which had capsized and sank that morning, with two of their crew. We gave them all they needed, and brought them safely to London.

In London, I was happy to be among my friends and my church once again. In November, my old friend, the famous Doctor Irving, bought a fine sloop of about 150 tons. He had a plan for a new adventure, cultivating a plantation on Jamaica on the Muskito Shore. He asked me to go with him, saying that he would trust me above anyone. With the advice of my friends, I accepted this offer. I knew that God's harvest was ripe in the West Indies. I hoped to be an instrument of God there, bringing some poor sinners to Jesus.

Before we left London, the Doctor and I met four Muskito Indians, who were chiefs in their own country, but who had been brought here by some English traders. One of them was the Muskito king's son, a youth of about eighteen years. He was baptised by the name of George. They were going back to Jamaica at the government's expense. They had been in England a year and had learned to speak pretty good English.

I came to talk to them a week before we sailed. I was troubled to discover that they had not been to church to be baptised, and that no care was shown for their morals. I took some of them to church before we sailed.

We sailed for Jamaica in November 1775, on board the sloop Morning Star, under Captain David Miller. During our voyage, I did all I could to teach the Indian prince about Christianity, which he knew nothing about. To my joy, he was interested and received the truths that God helped me to give him. In just eleven days, I taught him all the letters of the alphabet, and he could even put two or three of them together to spell words. I had Fox's Martyrology, and he asked many questions about the papal cruelties he saw in the pictures.

I made such progress with this young man in religion, that he would often pray with me. Before he ate with the gentlemen in the cabin, he would first come to me to pray. I was pleased with this and hoped for his conversion. Yet I knew that the devil, and his demons, would pull down as fast as I built up. In the end, the devil got the upper hand.

Some demons saw this poor heathen learning religion, laughed, and mocked him. This left the prince lost between two places. Some told him never to fear the devil, for he did not exist. They teased the poor innocent, so that he would not learn. Nor would pray with me.

In the end, he asked me, "How come all the white men on board who can read and write, and observe the sun, and know all things, yet they swear, lie, and get drunk, only excepting yourself?" I answered him that they did not fear God. If they died they could not be happy with God.

He replied that if they went to hell, he would go to hell too. I was sorry to hear this. He sometimes had a toothache, as did others on board. I asked him if their toothaches made his easier. He said, no. Then I told him that if he went to hell with them, their pains would not make his any lighter. This answer weighed on him. It depressed his spirits and he became fond of being alone.

When we were near Martinique, we had a brisk gale of wind. We had too much sail up, and the main mast went over the side. The yards, masts and rigging, came tumbling down on us, yet nobody was hurt - although some were a hair's width from being killed. I saw two men miraculously saved from being crushed.

On the 5th of January we saw Antigua and Montserrat, and we sailed along the rest of the islands. On the fourteenth, we arrived at Jamaica. One Sunday while we were there I took the Muskito Prince George to church, where he saw the sacrament administered. When we came out, there were all kinds of people buying and selling all kinds of things, for half a mile down to the waterside. I then taught him about the sabbath, and how no work should be done.

Once our ship was ready to sail for the Muskito shore, I went with the Doctor on board a ship from Guinea, to buy some slaves to take with us, to help cultivate a plantation. All those I chose were my own countrymen. On the 12th of February we sailed from Jamaica, and on the 18h, we arrived on the Muskito shore, at a place called Dupeupy.

All our Indian guests said farewell, and went ashore, where they met the Muskito king. We never saw them again. We then sailed to the southward of the shore, to a place called Cape Gracias a Dios, where three fine, large rivers flowed into a lagoon. The lagoon was full of fish and tortoises. Some native Indians came aboard and we treated them well. We told them that we had come to live among them, which they were happy to hear.

The Doctor, myself and some others went ashore with them. They took us to different places to see the land, to choose a place to make a plantation. We decided on a spot near a river bank, with rich soil. We took all we needed from the sloop, and began to clear the woods and plant vegetables, which grew quickly.

While we were busy with this work, our ship sailed north to the Black River to trade. While she was there, a Spanish ship took her. This made life difficult for us. However, we went on farming the land. We used to make fires all around us each night, to keep the wild beasts away. As soon it was dark, they roared horribly each night.

As our huts were deep in the woods, we often saw different kinds of animals. None of them hurt us, except the poisonous snakes. However, the Doctor used cured snakebites by giving the victim half a glass of strong rum, with Cayenne pepper in it. In this way, he cured two natives and one of his own slaves.

The Indians were very fond of the Doctor, and they had good reason. They never had such an useful man among them before. They came to us from all parts of the island. Some *woolwow*, or flat-headed Indians, who lived fifty or sixty miles above our river, brought us a good deal of silver in exchange for our goods.

The most useful things we got from the neighbouring Indians were turtle oil, shells, silk grass, and food. They would not do any work for us, except fishing. Just a few times, they helped us to cut some trees down, to build our houses. They cut trees exactly like Africans, with the work shared by men, women, and children. I do not think that any of the men had more than two wives. The wives were always with their husbands when they called to us. The women usually carried whatever they brought to us to trade, and always squatted down behind their husbands.

Whenever we gave them anything to eat, the men and their wives ate separately. They were modest and chaste. The women wore beads, and were fond of painting themselves. The men also painted both their faces and shirts. Their favourite colour is red. The women generally farm the land, while the men are all fishermen and canoe makers.

I never saw any nation that was so simple in their manners as these people, or who had such plain houses. Nor did they swear. The worst word I ever heard them say when quarrelling, was, "you rascal" – which they had learned from the English.

I never saw them worship God, but in respect, they were no worse than their European neighbours. There was not one white person in the area who was more pious than the Indians. The Europeans either worked or slept on Sunday. Sadly, we did the same, and we soon did not know one day from another. This way of living later made me think of leaving our camp.

The natives are well made and warlike. They are proud that they were never conquered by the Spaniards. They are great drinkers of strong liquor, when they can get it for them. We used to distil rum from pineapples, which were very plentiful there. When we had rum, we could not get the Indians away from our camp.

Yet they seemed more honest than any other nation I knew. As this country is hot, we lived in an open shed, where we kept had all kinds of goods. We had no door or lock, yet we slept in safety. Nothing was ever taken. This surprised us and we used to say that if we slept in this way in Europe, we would have our throats cut on the first night.

At certain times of the year, the Indian governor travels about and settles all the disputes among the people, like a judge. He is treated with great respect. He told us he was coming to our camp, by sending his stick ahead as a gift. In exchange, we sent him rum, sugar, and gunpowder. We then prepared to receive the governor and his people. When he came with his tribe, and all our neighbouring chieftains, we expected to find him a serious and solid judge. Yet instead, long before he and his gang came in sight, we heard their noise. They had taken some of the liquor we'd given to our neighbouring Indians.

When they arrived, we did not know what to make of our guests at first, and we would gladly have been rid of them. However, as we had little choice, we feasted with them all day, until the evening when the governor got quite drunk and became very unruly. He even hit one of our most friendly local chiefs and also took his gold-laced hat from him. At this, a great commotion broke out, but the Doctor made peace.

In the end, they became so outrageous that the Doctor left the house, and went to the nearest wood, leaving me to do as well as I could with them. I was so enraged with the Governor, that I could have wished him tied to a tree and flogged for his behaviour, but I didn't have enough people to cope with his gang.

I therefore thought of a strategy to quieten the riot. I remembered reading about Columbus, when he was among the Indians in Mexico or Peru. One time, he frightened them by telling them of events in the heavens. I tried the same trick, and it succeeded beyond my wildest dreams. I went to them, and took hold of the Governor. I pointed up to the heavens. I put them in fear, telling them God lived there and that he was angry with them. I said they must not quarrel and that they were all brothers. I said if they did not stop and go away quietly, I would take the book - pointing to the Bible - read, and *tell* God to make them dead. This worked like magic. The clamour immediately ceased. I gave them some rum and a few other things and they away peacefully. The Governor even gave our neighbour back his hat.

When the Doctor returned, he was pleased by my success in getting rid of our guests. The Muskito people near us even arranged celebrations to honour the Doctor, myself and our people. These celebrations called in their language *tourrie* or *dryckbot*. This translates as a feast of drinking about. Their drink is made of roasted pineapples, and casades chewed or beaten in mortars. After being left for some time, this ferments into a liquor. We had plenty of notice of the party. A white family, who lived within five miles of us, told us how the drink was made. Myself and two others went to the village where the party was to be held, and saw the way the drink was made. We also saw the animals that were to be eaten there. I cannot say that the sight of either the drink or the meat was enticing to me.

They had thousands of pineapples roasting, which they squeezed, dirt and all, into a canoe. The drink was kept in barrels and it looked exactly like hogwash. Men, women, and children were busy roasting the pineapples and squeezing them with their hands. For food, they had many tortoises and some dried turtle.

They also had three large alligators which were kept alive, tied to trees. I asked the people what they were going to do with the alligators and I was told they were to be eaten. I was surprised at this and went home a little disgusted.

When the day of the feast came, we took some rum with us. There was a great crowd of the Muskito people, who welcomed us kindly. The fun had begun before we came. They were dancing and playing music. Their musical instruments were nearly the same as those of any other dark people, although I thought these less melodious.

They made many strange gestures when dancing. These strange body postures were not too attractive to me. The males and females danced separately. The Doctor went to dance with the women's party, but the women were disgusted and so he joined the males.

At night, there were fireworks of a sort, made by setting fire to many pine trees. The dryckbot was passed around merrily, although there was more eating than drinking in it.

The oldest man in the area, Owden, was dressed in a strange and terrifying way. His body was wrapped with skins adorned with feathers. On his head, he wore a very high hat, with prickles like a porcupine. He made a certain noise which sounded like the cry of an alligator.

Our people danced amongst them to be kind. Some of our people could not drink their liquor, but our rum had enough customers, and it was soon gone. The alligators were killed and some of them were roasted. They roast food by digging a hole in the earth, and filling it with wood, which they burn to charcoal. They then lay sticks across this firepit, on which they place the meat. I had a raw piece of the alligator, which was very rich. I thought it looked like fresh salmon. Although it had a fragrant smell, I couldn't eat any of it. This merry making ended without the slightest argument, although there were many different nations and complexions there.

The rainy season begins about the end of May. It continued to rain heavily until August, when the rivers overflowed and many of our provisions were washed away. I thought this might have happened because we worked on Sundays, and this thought pained me.

I often wished to leave this place and sail for Europe. This crude and heathen way of living bothered me. The word of God says, '"What does it avail a man if he gain the whole world, but loses his own soul?" This question weighed on my mind. I did not know how to ask the doctor if I could leave, but I didn't want to stay any longer.

In June, I worked up the courage enough to ask him if I could leave. At first, he was unwilling to let me go, but I persuaded him in the end. He gave me the following certificate of good behaviour:

'The bearer, Gustavus Vassa, has served me several years with strict honesty, sobriety, and fidelity. I can, therefore, with justice recommend him for these qualifications; and indeed in every respect I consider him as an excellent servant. I do hereby certify that he always behaved well, and that he is perfectly trust-worthy.

'Charles Irving.'

Muskito Shore, June 15, 1776.

Although I was fond of the doctor, I was happy when he let me go. I got everything ready for my departure and hired some Indians with a large canoe to carry me away. All my poor countrymen, the slaves, were sad when they heard I was leaving. I had always treated them with care and affection. I did what I could to comfort the poor creatures, and make their lives easier.

On the 18th of June I bade a final farewell, and the doctor and I travelled south about twenty miles along the river. There I arranged passage on a sloop which was going to Jamaica. When the doctor and I parted, we both shed tears. The ship then sailed along the river until night, when she anchored in a lagoon in the river.

During the night, a schooner belonging to the same owners sailed in, looking for crew. Hughes, the owner of the sloop, asked me to go in the schooner as a sailor, saying he would pay me. I thanked him, but I said I wanted to go to Jamaica. He then immediately changed his tone, and swore, and abused me, asking how I came to be freed. I told him, and said that I come there with Dr. Irving, whom he had seen that day. This was of no use. He still swore at me, and cursed my old master as a fool who sold me my freedom. He said the doctor was another fool for letting me go from him.

He then told me to go in the schooner, saying that if I didn't I would not leave the sloop as a free man. I said this was very harsh, and begged to be put ashore, but he refused. I said I had been twice amongst the Turks, and had never received such treatment from them. I said I should not expect this sort of behaviour from Christians.

This angered him hugely and, with a volley of oaths, he replied, "Christians! Damn you, you are one of St. Paul's men but, by God, unless you have St. Paul's or St. Peter's faith, and walk upon the water to the shore, you shall not go out of this ship". I was now told this ship was going to Cartagena, where he swore he would sell me as a slave.

I simply asked him, "what right have you to sell me?" Without another word, he had some of his crew tie ropes around my ankles and wrists, and another rope went round my body. They then hoisted me off the ground. I was strung up, without judge or jury, merely because I was a free man, and because I could not get justice in this part of the world.

I was in terrible pain, and cried and begged mercy, but it was in vain. My tyrant, in a great rage, brought a musket out of the cabin, and loaded it in front me and the crew, and swore he would shoot me if I cried any more. I remained silent, seeing that not one white man on board had said a word on my behalf.

I hung in that way from ten o'clock at night until about one in the morning. When I saw that my cruel abuser was fast asleep, I begged some of his slaves to slack the rope that was round my body, so that my feet might rest on something. They did this at the risk of cruel punishment by their master, who had already beaten them for not tying me up fast enough when he commanded them.

I hung this way until six o'clock in the morning. I prayed for God to forgive this man, who cared not what he did. Yet when he woke in the morning, he was in the very same mood. When they took up the anchor, and the ship got under way, I again cried and begged to be released. As I was hung in the way of the sails they needed, they had to release me. When I got down, I spoke to a carpenter I knew on board about what was done to me. He also knew the doctor, and the good opinion he had of me.

This man then went to the captain, and told him not to carry me away as I was the doctor's steward. He said the doctor regarded me highly, and would be resent this if he found out about it. At this, the captain told a young man to put me ashore in a small canoe I had brought with me. I rushed into the canoe and set off, while the tyrant owner was below in his cabin. Yet he saw me in the canoe, when I was just thirty or forty yards from the ship. He ran on the deck with a loaded musket in his hand, aimed at me, and swore that he would shoot me if I didn't come back on board.

As I knew he would have done as he said, I went back to the ship again. Just as I came alongside, he began abusing the captain for letting me go. The captain argued back, and they soon got into a heated argument. The young man that was with me got out of the canoe while the vessel sailed fast on a smooth sea.

I then thought it was now or never, and so I set off again in the canoe - paddling for my life towards the shore. Thankfully, the confusion was so great on board, that I got out of reach of musket shot unnoticed, while the vessel sailed on quickly in a different direction, so that they could not catch me without tacking.

I got to shore, and told the other owner how I had been treated. He was astonished, and seemed very sorry for what had happened. He gave me some refreshment and Indian corn for my voyage of about eighteen miles south, to look for another ship.

He then directed me to a local Indian chief, known as the admiral, who had once been at our camp. I set off alone in the canoe across a large lagoon, although though I was weary, and had pains in my gut, thanks to the ropes I had hung from the night before. At times, I couldn't to manage the canoe, as the paddling was hard. However, a little before dark I got to the Indian village, where some of the Indians knew me and received me kindly.

I asked for the admiral and they took me to his house. He was glad to see me, and gave me what he had for comfort. I was given a hammock to sleep in. They treated me more like Christians than the whites I was with the night before did, even though they were not baptised.

I told the admiral that I wanted to go to the next port to find a ship to take me to Jamaica. I said that he could take my canoe as payment. He agreed, and sent five able Indians with a large canoe to carry me to the port, which was fifty miles away.

We set off the next morning. We paddled out of the lagoon and went along shore, where sea was so high that the canoe was often nearly filled with water. We had to go ashore in places, and drag the canoe across the land. We spent two nights in the swamps, which swarmed with mosquitos.

This hard journey over land and water ended on the third day, when I went on board a sloop commanded by one Captain Jenning. She was partly loaded, and he told me he was expecting to sail for Jamaica any day. He agreed for me to work my passage to Jamaica.

We soon sailed, but I had again been tricked. We sailed southward along the Muskito shore, instead of steering for Jamaica. I was made to help cut great deal of mahogany wood on the shore as we coasted along it, and I had to load the vessel with it before she sailed on.

I had to carry on working, as I did not know how escape these liars. I thought patience was the only remedy I had left. There was much work but little food on board, unless we caught turtles. On this coast, there was also a fish called a manatee, which is excellent to eat as its flesh is more like beef than fish. Its scales are as large as a shilling coin, and its skin is thicker than any other fish. However, in the brackish waters along shore, there are large numbers of alligators, which made the fish scarce.

I was on the sloop sixteen days, when we met a smaller sloop called the Indian Queen, commanded by John Baker. He was an Englishman, who had been working this coast a long time, trading turtle for shells and silver. He had a good quantity of goods on board. Yet he badly needed crew and, knowing I was a free man who wanted to go to Jamaica, he told me if he could get one or two crew, that he would sail immediately for that island.

He made out to be respectful to me, and promised me forty-five shillings sterling a month if I would sail with him. I thought this much better than cutting wood for nothing. I therefore told the other captain that I wanted to go to Jamaica on the other ship. But he would not listen to me and, he got the vessel ready to sail, planning to carry me away against my will.

I immediately called for the Indian Queen's boat to come, as I had arranged. The boat came alongside and a former shipmate from my North Pole expedition helped me get my things into the boat. I went on board of the Indian Queen on July the 10th 1776. A few days later, we sailed. Yet again, instead of going to Jamaica as the captain had promised me, the vessel went south, trading along the coast. I had been tricked yet again, but worst of all, he turned out to be a cruel and bloody minded man, and a horrid blasphemer.

He had a white pilot, Stoker, whom he beat often as severely as he did some of the black people he had on board. One night, after he had beaten this man most cruelly, he put him into the boat, and made two of the black men row Stoker to a small, desolate island. He loaded two pistols, and swore he would shoot the black men if they brought Stoker on board again.

There was no doubt but he would do as he said. The two poor fellows had to obey this cruel order. Yet the captain was asleep, the two black men took a blanket and carried it to poor Stoker, which I believe saved his life from the insects. A great deal of persuasion was needed before the captain would let Stoker come back on board. When he did come, he was very ill. He remained sick until he drowned a little time afterward.

As we sailed southward, we came to many uninhabited islands. These were overgrown with fine large coconut trees. Needing food, I brought a boat load of these on board, which were delicious, and lasted us for weeks.

One day, I had been on board a whole day without food. I made signals for boats to come from the shore, but nobody came. I then prayed to God for help, and at dark of the evening I went below decks. Just as I lay down, I heard a strange noise on the deck, and went back up to see what it was. What dud I see but a fine large fish about seven or eight pounds, which had jumped aboard! I took it , thanked God, and amazingly the captain did not take it from me. Just him and I were on board as the rest had gone ashore trading.

Sometimes, the crew did not come back for days. This used to worry the captain, and then he would vent his fury by beating me, or in other cruel ways. One day, in his wild, mad life, he hit me several times with different things. He struck me across my mouth, with a burning red stick from the fire. He then put a barrel of gunpowder on the deck, and swore that he would blow up the ship. I was at my wit's end, and prayed for God to guide me.

The barrel was open, and the captain took a lighted stick out of the fire to blow us up, because there was a ship coming in, which he thought was Spanish. He was afraid of falling into their hands. I took an axe, without him noticing, and put myself between him and the powder. I decided to cut him down if he tried to light the barrel. I spent over an hour in this situation. He struck me often, and kept the fire in his hand all that time. In any other part of the world, it would have been justifiable to kill him. I prayed to God, who gave me a focused mind. God restrained my hand and helped in this time of need. The captain's fury began to ease as night approached.

The next morning, we discovered that the ship which had awoken such fury in the captain was in fact an English sloop. It soon came to anchor near where we were, and I learned that Doctor Irving was on board, on his way from the Muskito shore to Jamaica. I wanted to immediately go to my friend, but the captain would not let me leave the ship. I then told the doctor, by letter, how I was treated, and begged him to take me with him. The doctor said that this was not in his power, as he was a passenger. He sent me some rum and sugar.

I then found out what had happened after I had left the land I managed for the doctor on the Muskito shore. I had made sure the slaves were well fed and comfortable. However, a white overseer took my place and this man inhumanly beat and cut the slaves. As a result, they all got into a large canoe and tried to escape. Not knowing where to go, or how to paddle the canoe, they were all drowned. The doctor's plantation was now left uncultivated, and he was now going to Jamaica to buy more slaves and stock for it.

On the 14th of October, the Indian Queen arrived at Kingston in Jamaica. When we were unloaded I demanded my wages, which amounted to eight pounds and five shillings sterling. Captain Baker refused to give me a penny, although it was the hardest money I had ever earned in my life. I told Doctor Irving about this, and he did all he could to help me get my money. We went to all nine magistrates in Kingston, but they all refused to do anything for me, and said my oath could not be allowed against a white man. Not only that, but Baker threatened to beat me severely for attempting to get my money. He would have done this, except that the doctor arranged for me to go under the protection of Captain Douglas of the man of war, the Squirrel.

It was common practice in Jamaica not to pay free black men for their labour. One day, I went with a free black tailor, named Joe Diamond, to one Mr. Cochran, who owed him a small sum of money. Cochrane immediately took a horse-whip to pay him with. With the help of a good pair of heels, the tailor ran off. Oppression such as this made me seek a ship to get off the island as fast as I could. By the mercy of God, that November, I found a ship bound for England.

Before I left Jamaica, I bade a final farewell to the good doctor. When I left Jamaica, he was busy refining sugar. Some months after I arrived in England I learned, with sorrow, that my friend was dead. He had died after eating some bad fish.

We had many heavy gales of wind on our passage to England. The main event of the voyage was that an

American privateer was captured and burned by his Majesty's ship the Squirrel. On the 7th of January, 1777, we arrived at Plymouth. I was happy to walk upon English ground again. After spending some happy times in Plymouth and Exeter with some of my godly friends, I went to London, with a heart full of thanks for God's mercies.

CHAPTER 12

AFTER 1777

This was my life until the year 1777. From then on, my life became more sedate. I had become disgusted with the seafaring life, since I had suffered so much injustice around the world. I decided not to return to the sea, at least for some time. I found steady work as a servant soon after I returned to London.

Soon after I arrived in London, I saw an extraordinary thing, which sheds light on the African skin tone. A white African woman, who I had seen before in London, had married a white man. She had three boys, and they were all mixed race, although they had light hair.

In 1779, I went to work as a servant for Governor MacNamara, who had spent much time on the African coast. I used to often ask the other servants to join me in prayer, but they only mocked me for this. However, when the Governor learned that I was of a religious mind, he asked what religion I belonged to. I told him I was a protestant of the Church of England, who believed in the thirty-nine articles of that church.

A few days later, we spoke again about faith. He said that, if I wished, he could get me sent out as a missionary to

Africa, where I might convert my countrymen to the Gospel. At first, I refused. I told him how I had been treated on my last voyage to Jamaica, when I tried to convert the Indian prince. I said that I imagined Africans would not welcome me either, if I tried to preach there. He told me not to fear, as he would apply to the Bishop of London to get me ordained a priest. I agreed to go to Africa if supported by the church. I hoped I might do some good for my countrymen.

We immediately wrote to the Bishop of London, explaining the plan. I wrote a fine letter, explaining that I wished to serve as a missionary priest in Africa to help bring Christianity to the region. My employer, Mr MacNamara, wrote that he had lived on the coast of Africa for seven years, and believed the plan would meet with success. He also wrote that he knew "a very respectable character, a black priest at Cape Coast Castle". He also wrote, "I know the within named Gustavus Vassa, and believe him a moral good man."

Our letters to the Lord Bishop were also sent with a letter from a Dr Wallace, who had also lived in Africa for many years. The good doctor wrote that he supported our plan and suggested that the bishop should support it too. I met with the bishop, who spoke to me politely about this plan, but said he would not ordain me. I tell this story because it shows that gentlemen of good sense and education believe that Africa could be converted to Christianity.

Shortly after this, I left the Governor. I then worked for a nobleman in the Devonshire militia. I was with him in the military camp at Coxheath for some time.

In the year 1783, I visited eight counties in Wales, as I was curious about that country. I went down into a coal-pit in Shropshire out of interest, but my curiosity nearly cost me my life. While I was in the pit, the coals fell in and buried one poor man, who was nearby. I got out as fast as I could, having learned that the surface of the earth is the safest part of it.

In the spring of 1784, I began to think of going out on the old ocean once again. I soon joined a fine new ship called the London, commanded by Captain Martin Hopkin. We sailed to New York. I admired that fine city, which is large and well built, with abundant goods for sale. While we lay in New York harbour, a strange thing happened. One day, a criminal was to be hanged at the gallows, but with the condition that if any woman married the man under the gallows, his life would to be spared. A woman came up, and the marriage ceremony took place, saving the man.

Once our ship was loaded, we sailed back to London in January 1785. The captain was a good man, and so I sailed with him again that spring. In March 1785, we set out for Philadelphia. On the 5th of April, we passed Land's End, with a pleasant gale behind us. At about nine o'clock that night, the moon shone bright, and the sea was smooth. Our ship was running before the wind, at four or five knots.

At this time, another ship was coming against us at the same speed. Nobody on either ship saw the other until we crashed into each other, head to head. She did great damage to our ship, but I think we did worse to her. As we passed by each other, they called to us to stop and launch our boat, but we had enough to do to save ourselves. Within a few minutes, we saw no more of her. We repaired our ship as best as we could the next day, and continued our voyage to America.

In May, we arrived at Philadelphia. I was glad to see this lovely old town once more. I was delighted to see the good Quakers freeing slaves and easing the burdens of my oppressed fellow Africans. It lifted my heart when one of these kind people brought me to see a free school they had set up for black people. Through this, they became educated and productive members of society.

Along with good work in educating black people, and campaigning against slavery, some Quakers had written a book called *A Caution to Great Britain and her Colonies, concerning the Calamitous State of the enslaved Negroes.*

In October 1785 I and some fellow Africans gave a speech of thanks to the Quakers in Lombard Street, London, as follows:

"We the poor, oppressed, needy, and much-degraded negroes, desire to approach you with this address of thanks, with our inmost love and warmest acknowledgment; and with the deepest sense of your

benevolence, unwearied labour, and kind interposition, towards breaking the yoke of slavery, and to administer a little comfort and ease to thousands and tens of thousands of very grievously afflicted, and too heavy burthened negroes.

"Gentlemen, could you, by perseverance, at last be enabled, under God, to lighten in any degree the heavy burthen of the afflicted, no doubt it would, in some measure, be the possible means, under God, of saving the souls of many of the oppressors; and, if so, sure we are that the God, whose eyes are ever upon all his creatures, and always rewards every true act of virtue, and regards the prayers of the oppressed, will give to you and yours those blessings which it is not in our power to express or conceive, but which we, as a part of those captived, oppressed, and afflicted people, most earnestly wish and pray for."

These gentlemen received us very kindly, and promised to keep working to help he oppressed Africans. I was also invited to a Quaker's wedding, where I saw their simple yet moving ceremonies.

We returned to London in August. As our ship was not going to sea for a while, I went on board an American ship called the Harmony, as a steward. Under Captain John Willets, we left London in March 1786, bound for Philadelphia. Eleven days after we sailed, our forward mast came down in a gale. As we then had less sail, our voyage took nine weeks, and the market for our goods was bad when we arrived. To make matters worse, the captain began to play tricks on me, like those often played on free black people in the West Indies. Thankfully, I had many friends in Philadelphia, who helped to protect me.

When I returned to London in August, I was surprised to find that the British government had plans to send some Africans home to their native land, and that ships were ready to carry them to Sierra Leone. I was delighted to hear of this humane plan.

In London, there was a charitable committee to support the black poor. I was known to some of its members and, when they heard of my arrival, they sent for me. When I arrived, we spoke about the government's plan. They thought I was qualified to manage parts of the effort, and asked me to go with the black poor to Africa.

I wasn't sure about this and told them I was worried about opposition from the slave dealers there. However, the gentlemen persuaded me to go, and recommended me to the Commissioners of his Majesty's Navy. In November 1786, I was appointed Commissary for the British government for the expedition. I received my formal written warrant and orders, which were as follows:

"To Mr. Gustavus Vassa,
 Commissary of Provisions and
 Stores for the Black Poor
 going to Sierra Leone.

*By the principal Officers and Commissioners of
his Majesty's Navy.*

*Whereas you were directed, by our warrant of the 4th of
last month, to receive into your charge from Mr. Irving
the surplus provisions remaining of what was provided for
the voyage, as well as the provisions for the support of the
black poor, after the landing at Sierra Leone, with the
cloathing, tools, and all other articles provided at
government's expense; and as the provisions were laid in
at the rate of two months for the voyage, and for four
months after the landing, but the number embarked being
so much less than was expected, whereby there may be a
considerable surplus of provisions, cloathing, &c. These
are, in addition to former orders, to direct and require you
to appropriate or dispose of such surplus to the best
advantage you can for the benefit of government, keeping
and rendering to us a faithful account of what you do
herein. And for your guidance in preventing any white
persons going, who are not intended to have the
indulgences of being carried thither, we send you
herewith a list of those recommended by the Committee
for the black poor as proper persons to be permitted to
embark, and acquaint you that you are not to suffer any
others to go who do not produce a certificate from the
committee for the black poor, of their having their
permission for it. For which this shall be your warrant.
Dated at the Navy Office, January 16, 1787.*

J. HINSLOW,
GEO. MARSH,
W. PALMER. "

I quickly went about my duty on board the ships. Yet when I worked for the government, I saw flagrant abuses committed by the agent, which I tried to stop. To give one example, the government had ordered 750 slop buckets for the voyage. Yet I could only find 426. When I asked for the rest, it seemed they had never been bought - although they had been paid for by government.

What was worse, the accommodation for the poor black people was wretched. Many had no beds, clothes or other essentials. When the agent did nothing to remedy these issues, in February 1787 I asked Captain Thompson, of the Nautilus to stand as a witness to this injustice. I arranged for a letter setting out these poor conditions to be published in the Morning Herald on the 4th of February. This was signed by twenty of the African chiefs.

I could not silently let government to be cheated, and my African countrymen mistreated, and left destitute. I therefore told the Commissioners of the Navy of the agent's misdeeds. Soon after this, an influential man in the city had me dismissed from my role, by telling lies about me. This same man had plans to profit by taking passengers on the voyage, at the government's expense. I was dismissed even though I knew the commissioners were happy with my work, as they had written to Captain Thompson to say so.

The voyage to Sierra Leone went ahead. But many of the Africans were worn out by their ill treatment. Many became sick thanks to the lack of medicine, clothes and bedding on board. They reached Sierra Leone just as the rainy season began. At that time of year, it is impossible to grow crops. Their provisions soon ran out. Many had been cooped up in the ships in poor conditions for eight long months, from October to June. It is no surprise that many died soon after they arrived.

So ended my part in the much talked of expedition to Sierra Leone. It ended terribly, even though its aims were humane. Its failure was not the government's fault, but was thanks to mismanagement and corruption.

I explain all this as the expedition was the subject of much public criticism. Some even took delight at my being dismissed. It seems strange that anyone would take delight in the misfortune of another, but I wish to stand by my own integrity, and not hide behind the wrongdoing of another.

On May 12, 1787 I wrote to the Commissioners of the Navy after I had been dismissed. I noted that they had not given any reason for my dismissal. I said I was at a loss to understand why they had suddenly changed their good opinion of me. I told them I had reason to believe that I had been lied about, because of my efforts to prevent corruption. I also explained that I had lost what little I had in preparing myself for the expedition. I asked for this, and my wages due.

I received no reply, but their lordships did send me the princely sum of £50 sterling a few months later. I take this as proof that they knew I had done my job honestly and well.

On the 21st of March, 1788, I had the honour of presenting the Queen with a letter on behalf of my African countrymen. As King George III was ill at the time, the Queen took over many of his duties. I wrote "to beg her compassion for millions of my African countrymen, who groan under the lash of tyranny in the West Indies."

I wrote as the oppression and cruelty against slaves in the West Indies was then being considered by the British parliament. I noted that even some slaveowners in the West Indies were calling for the slave trade to be ended.

I begged her majesty to use her influence in favour of the Africans so that they might no longer be treated as animals. I told her that she could help bring happiness to millions, and be rewarded by their grateful prayers. I said that the new laws being made by assembly of Jamaica are proof of the cruelty of slavery in the West Indies. hope to live to see the British government one day give freedom and justice to the slaves, and so to honour the common nature of all humanity.

In my letter to the Queen, I also wrote that:

229

These injustices speak to every man of feeling and conscience. History will be kind to those noble few who act against slavery. That is why I hope and those in power will give their attention to these evils. This would prove that we have a free and generous government. To end slavery is to pursue greatness.

May the time come when the black people shall gratefully remember when their freedom was granted. Then shall those who stood for humanity be honoured.

May God make the British parliament givers of light, liberty, and science to the furthest parts of the earth. This will be a glory to God and it will bring peace and goodwill to men. Glory, honour, peace to every soul of man, who works for the good. It is goodness that raises a nation up, and evil which brings destruction.

If a system of commerce were established in Africa, the demand for goods would grow. The Africans would quickly adopt the British fashions, manners and customs, which would increase trade. The potential consumption of a continent, nearly twice as large as Europe, which is rich in agriculture and minerals, is incalculable.

The difference in consumption between the native Britons and this generation is infinite. It will be equally immense in Africa as civilisation advances. Commercial trade with Africa opens an huge source of wealth to the manufacturing interests of Great Britain. All this will more than make up for the loss of the slave trade, if it is banned.

The value of British manufacturing is becoming greater than agriculture. The abolition of slavery will help manufacturing to grown contrary to what many say. This is because manufacturers of this country will become busy supplying the African market.

Africa abounds in resources. Industry, enterprise and mining, will grow their as the continent develops. This process would open an endless field of commerce to British manufacturers and merchants, to the benefit of the whole country. The abolition of slavery would in reality a universal good for Britain.

Torture, murder, and every other imaginable barbarity are done to the slaves with impunity. I pray the slave trade will be abolished soon. If the manufacturing industry supports this cause, it can help it to be achieved. As I have said, it in their own interest - except for those who manufacture neck-yokes, collars, chains, hand-cuffs, leg-bolts, drags, thumb-screws, iron muzzles, coffins, whips - and other instruments of torture used in the slave trade.

I believe that soon, the growing feeling against slavery will prevail – out of self-interest as well out of justice and humanity. Europe has one hundred and twenty million people. How many million pf people does Africa have? If the Africans spend £5 a head each year on European goods, this could mean riches beyond imagination for Europe.

The facts speak for themselves. If the blacks were allowed to remain in their own country, they would double in number every fifteen years – as would the demand for goods. Cotton and indigo grow easily in most parts of Africa, which would also help to support the manufacturing towns of Great Britain. It is glorious to imagine the future trading possibilities of a continent ten thousand miles in circumference, which is immensely rich in materials and people.

■■■

I do not think there is much merit in my story. It was written by one who is both unwilling and unable to adorn the plain truth with the colour of imagination.

My life has been chequered and my adventures have been many. It may be that the things that happened to me are uninteresting to many people. I mention them only because they made an impression on my mind, and I learned from them.

Since I was a boy, I've looked for the hand of God in the smallest things. All that has happened to me has taught me lessons in morality and religion. That's why every story I've told was important to me. After all, if an event teaches us to become wiser, then it becomes important.

Those who see the world in this way can learn something from any book, and from even the smallest event in their lives. To others, the experience of many ages is of no use, since they refuse to learn anything from it. To offer such people the treasures of wisdom, is like throwing jewels into the sea.

Printed in Great Britain
by Amazon